## DEATH AND THE CHRISTIAN

**JOHN R. W. STOTT** shows that the living and the dead are not separated, but two parts of the great community of the Christian Church.

**ELISABETH ELLIOT** discusses the day-by-day experience of bereavement, its emotional depths and how it may be used to strengthen one's ties to life and to God.

**C. EVERETT KOOP** confronts the problems facing the parents of a child they know must die.

**MIRIAM G. MORAN** recalls a Christmas funeral, and the sudden understanding of the Christian victory over death.

**JOSEPH T. BAYLY** details the stages of approaching death and what they mean to family, friends, and the sufferer.

From pastoral and medical experience, from personal loss, from inner faith and deep Bible study, these and fifteen other leading Christian writers present advice, comfort and inspiration to help you deal with the most awesome and inescapable stage of human life, its ending—and its new beginning in Christ.

# DEATH: JESUS MADE IT ALL DIFFERENT

*Edited by*
MIRIAM G. MORAN

Keats Publishing, Inc.
New Canaan, Connecticut

We acknowledge with thanks the following permissions to publish:

"The Ones Who Are Left" by Elisabeth Elliot from *Christianity Today*. Copyright © 1976 by Elisabeth Elliot.

"A Time To Be Born and a Time To Die" by David H. Freeman, from *The Reformed Journal*, May-June, 1976. Copyright © 1976 by William B. Eerdmans Publishing Company.

"Mercy-Dying vs. Mercy-Killing" by Norman Geisler, from *Ethics: Alternatives and Issues*. Copyright © 1971 by Zondervan Publishing House. Reprinted by permission of the author.

"What Do I Say to Someone Who's Dying?" by Joseph T. Bayly, from *Moody Monthly*. Copyright © 1974 by Joseph T. Bayly.

**Death: Jesus Made It All Different**

A PIVOT BOOK published 1977
by arrangement with *Eternity Magazine*

Copyright © 1977 by *Eternity Magazine*

All rights reserved

Library of Congress Catalog Card Number: 76-587-68

Printed in the United States of America

PIVOT BOOKS are published by Keats Publishing, Inc.
36 Grove Street, New Canaan, Connecticut 06840

*To those who leave and those who are left*

# FOREWORD

About eight years ago, Dr. Elisabeth Kübler-Ross, a Swiss-born psychiatrist, interviewed more than 900 terminal patients and published an insightful book called *On Death and Dying*. Since then, death has become an acceptable subject. It is no longer taboo. It is no longer camouflaged by euphemisms. It still is not a pleasant subject, but at least people are talking about it. And wondering.

This little book is intended to help those who want to know what others have thought and said about death. It is a handbook of advice and information.

Some chapters deal with the difficult subject of prolonging life by artificial means. Is that always required? Some chapters weigh the emotions of the dying and the bereaved. Others are concerned with suicide. Is it ever permissible? Some examine the funeral and other rituals which take place after a death. Others are a close study of pertinent Scripture passages. Just what does the Bible say about death and the life hereafter? And some discuss the sensitive ministry of comforting the bereaved.

The authors form a broad spectrum of viewpoints. They are doctors, pastors, theologians, teachers; they are parents, single people, husbands, wives. But they all have two things in common: 1) they have all been touched by death in some way, and 2) they have let the Bible help them. Consequently, each one looks at death from more than an earth-bound perspective. They have seen beyond the grave, and that colors the whole way they look at life on this side of the grave.

Read what they have to say. I think you'll like their perspective.

MIRIAM G. MORAN

# CONTENTS

1. DEATH: LIFE'S ONE AND ONLY CERTAINTY — 13
   *J. I. Packer*

2. BEYOND THE DIVIDE — 22
   *John R. W. Stott*

3. DEATH: JESUS MADE IT ALL DIFFERENT — 27
   *Gordon Chilvers*

4. THE LAST SAY — 33
   *Miriam G. Moran*

5. SORROW WITH HOPE — 37
   *Donald Grey Barnhouse*

6. THE ONES WHO ARE LEFT — 42
   *Elisabeth Elliot*

7. A TIME TO BE BORN AND A TIME TO DIE — 51
   *David H. Freeman*

8. MERCY-DYING VS. MERCY-KILLING — 57
   *Norman Geisler*

9. A DOCTOR SPEAKS FROM THE NURSING HOME — 60
   *Larry Edwards*

10. IS SUICIDE AN ANSWER? — 66
    *Ray C. Stedman*

11. HOW A CHRISTIAN FIGHTS SUICIDE — 71
    *Anonymous*

12. WHAT SHALL I TELL MY CHILD? — 79
    *Ellis Guthrie*

13. WHAT I TELL THE PARENTS OF A
    DYING CHILD                                    83
    *C. Everett Koop*

14. WHAT DO I SAY TO SOMEONE WHO'S
    DYING?                                         91
    *Joseph T. Bayly*

15. HOW NOT TO BE A MISERABLE COMFORTER    101
    *Marjorie Brumme*

16. OUR STRANGE WAYS OF DEATH               105
    *Bob W. Brown and Henry A. Buchanan*

17. DON'T SHORT-CIRCUIT GRIEF               113
    *Robert James St. Clair*

18. TWO VIEWS ON TODAY'S FUNERAL
    CUSTOMS:
        I. SORROWING AS THOSE WHO
           HAVE HOPE                        120
           *Roger F. Campbell*
       II. A TIME TO MOURN                  126
           *Eleanor Harker*

19. HOW CHRISTIAN ARE OUR FUNERALS?         131
    *Frances Tucker*

20. GRANDMA'S FUNERAL: PAINFUL
    POSTMORTEM                              136
    *Bruce R. Reichenbach*

# DEATH: JESUS MADE IT ALL DIFFERENT

Chapter 1

# *DEATH: LIFE'S ONE AND ONLY CERTAINTY*

By J. I. Packer

"He passed, however, a not unsuccessful life in his profession, and the only Intruder he found himself unable to deal with was death."

These words of Novelist Charles Williams would make an epitaph for many today, for they state very accurately how death hits the natural man. It does in truth come as an *intruder*, uninvited and not bargained for. And when a man sees it coming, panic rises. However brave or blasé a face he may put on it, inwardly he feels isolated, paralyzed, drained of strength. He really is unable to cope with it.

All the world over, people get embarrassed and rattled if you talk to them about dying. Everywhere, the experience of bereavement, or the death of a friend, shakes people to the core; everywhere, the expectation of dying casts invalids into apathetic despair.

Nineteen times the Bible calls the prospect of death its "shadow." We see death looming up ahead of us as a gross, dark threat, casting a shadow before it, streaking our sunniest moments already with chill and gloom. Daily we advance towards it; soon its shadow will engulf us completely, and life's sunshine will be over for ever. What lies beyond the darkness? When this life stops—what starts?

Some, of course, resolutely shrug it off. To think about death, they say, is morbid; healthy-minded people will not do it. But I doubt if this is the wisest attitude to take. In the first place, to reckon with death is no more than sober realism, since death is life's one and only certainty.

Philip of Macedon was wise when he charged a slave to remind him every morning: "Philip, remember that thou must die."

Perhaps young people are better able to think straight about death than any other class of people.

Members of this age-group see death as an unnatural evil, a cosmic outrage, making a mockery of all their newborn longings after truth, beauty, and achievement. Doubt gnaws: Is there any sense in pursuing worthwhile objectives, if at the end of your quest, or before it, you have to die?

As a rule, it is only in youth that this sense of the outrageousness of death is strong. By middle age, youth's vision is blurred, and one simply resigns oneself to dying in due course, as a natural necessity (though one does not come to love death on that account). By old age, the vision is almost forgotten, and physical vitality falls so low that death may even be welcomed as a release.

When a person dies of disease or old age, we call it "natural death," reserving "unnatural death" for cases of accident and foul play. But Scripture confirms our instinctive feeling that, in the deepest sense, all death is unnatural.

What is death? It is a dissolving of the union between spirit and body. "Then shall the dust return to the earth . . . and the spirit . . . unto God who gave it" (Eccl. 12:7). There is a reference here to the story of creation. As in the beginning God made man by breathing life into a thing of dust, so now in death He partly unmakes him, severing the two realities which He originally joined together. This disintegration is, to man, unnatural in the highest degree.

That is why sensitive people find dead bodies uncanny. It is sometimes said that the dead look peaceful, but this is hardly correct. What is true is that corpses look *vacant*. It is their evident emptiness that we find unnerving—the sense that the person whose body and face this was is simply *gone*.

Does death mean personal annihilation? Indeed no. Death is, in Paul's phrase, an "unclothing" of a person by dismantling his earthly "tent," but it is not the end of his personal life. The Bible everywhere takes personal survival for granted. The Old Testament pictures the dead as going "down" (a natural metaphor) to the place which it calls *Sheol* (*Hades* in the Septuagint and Greek New Testament). The Authorized Version renders both Sheol and Hades as "hell," but this is misleading, since neither term implies anything as to the happiness or unhappiness of the inhabitants of this place.

Sheol is not, however, the ultimate abode of the dead. Scripture looks forward to an emptying of Hades when the dead are raised bodily for judgment at Christ's return (John 5:28f.; Rev. 20:12f.; cf. Dan. 12:2f.). Those whose names are written in the book of life will then be welcomed into endless bliss, but the rest will undergo the extremest manifestation of divine displeasure.

This is described in various texts throughout the New Testament as unquenchable fire; Gehenna—which was the place of incineration outside Jerusalem—where the devouring worm never dies; a place of wailing and gnashing of teeth; eternal punishment; everlasting fire, prepared for the devil and his angels; indignation and wrath, tribulation and anguish; everlasting destruction from the presence of the Lord; and the lake which burneth with fire and brimstone.

Some hold that these texts imply the annihilation of those rejected—one searing moment in the fire, and then oblivion. But it seems clear that in reality the "second death" is no more a cessation of being than is the first. For one thing, the word rendered "destruction" in II Thessalonians 1:9 (*olethros*) means, not annihilation, but *ruin* (cf. its use in I Thess. 5:3).

Secondly, the insistence in these texts that the fire, punishment, and destruction, are *eternal* (*aioniōs*, literally "age-long"), and that the worm in Gehenna is *undying*, would be pointless and inappropriate if all that is envisaged is momentary extinction; just as it would be pointless and inappropriate to dwell on "unending" pain resulting from an immediately fatal bullet wound. Either these words indicate the endlessness of torment, or they are superfluous and misleading.

Thirdly, to the argument that *aioniōs* means only "relating to the age to come," without any implications of endless duration, it seems sufficient to say that if in Matthew 25:46 "eternal" life means endless bliss (and surely it does), then the "eternal" punishment mentioned there must be endless too.

In the fourth place, we are told that in the "lake

of fire" the devil will be "tormented day and night for ever and ever" (Rev. 20:10). That any man sent to join him will endure a similar eternity of retribution is clear from the parallel language of Revelation 14:10f.: "he [the beast worshiper] shall be tormented with fire and brimstone ... the smoke of their torment ascendeth up for ever and ever; and they have no rest day nor night."

It seems plain that what these texts teach is not extinction, but the far worse prospect of an endless awareness of God's just and holy displeasure. Grievous as we may find it to contemplate, an endless hell can no more be removed from the New Testament than an endless heaven can. This is why physical death (the first death) is so fearful a prospect for Christless men: not because it means extinction, but precisely because it does *not* mean extinction, only the unending pain of the second death.

In the Old Testament, references to death denote on the surface, at any rate, only physical dissolution. But in the New Testament the concept of death is radically deepened. Death in the New Testament is seen primarily as a spiritual state, the state of mankind without Christ. As physical death means the separating of the spirit from the body, so spiritual death means a state in which man is separated from God, cut off from His favor and fellowship, "dead in trespasses and sins." As in the Bible "life" repeatedly denotes the joy of fellowship with God, so the state of being alienated from this "life of God" is equated with "death." It is from spiritual death first and foremost that we need to be delivered.

Throughout the Bible, death in both its physical and its spiritual aspects is viewed as a penal evil,

God's judgment upon sin. Death, says Paul, is the wages which are paid to sin's employees. When God told Adam, "in the day that thou eatest thereof [of the tree of knowledge] thou shalt surely die," the primary and explicit reference was to physical dissolution, as Genesis 3:19 makes clear. (The words "in the day that" seem to express no more than certainty of sequence, not necessarily temporal *immediacy*: cf. the use of the same phrase in I Kings 2:37.)

Thus, when Paul says that in Adam all die, the context shows that he has in mind physical mortality alone, which Christ is to abolish by raising the dead. But in Romans 5:12f., when he speaks of Christ delivering the "many" who are His from the "death" in which Adam had involved them, his reference is wider. For the deliverance he expounds is not physical resurrection merely (indeed, physical resurrection is not mentioned in the passage at all). It is, rather, present "justification" which will lead to a restoration of "life"—in other words, the healing of that vitiated relationship with God of which physical death was the proof and emblem.

The world usually refers to physical death merely as an ending, the closing of a door on one's earthly life; but the New Testament sees it also as a beginning—the opening of a door into our destiny, the new life in which we start to reap what we have sown.

In the Old Testament, it is true, we find the saints shrinking from the prospect of death, believing that in Sheol, though God was not absent, they could not hope for such close and sweet fellowship with Him as they had enjoyed on earth. The New Testament seems to hint that the Old Testament saints were in fact kept waiting until Christ Him-

## Death: Life's One and Only Certainty 19

self entered Sheol (the "descent into hell" of the Creed: cf. Acts 2:27f.) before their fellowship with God in the celestial Zion became the complete and perfect thing that it is now (cf. Heb. 11:40 with 12:18–23).

However that may be, it is made clear in the New Testament that in these "last days" the wheels of divine repayment are revolving from the moment of death on, and that each man at once finds himself experiencing in intensified form that relationship with God and with His Christ which he chose to have during his life in this world—either to be *with* God and Christ, which now proves to be Paradise and joy, or else to remain *without* both in the spiritual darkness of a self-willed and self-centered existence—a condition which now, as one begins to realize what one has lost, proves to be agony.

For those with Christ, God in grace makes the new life one of increasing joy without any further pain; for those without Christ, God in retributive justice makes the new life one of increasing pain without any further joy.

But it is too late to change; after death there is a "great gulf" fixed between those whom God accepts and those whom He rejects. The time of choice has passed. All that remains now is to receive the consequences of the choice already made.

There is nothing arbitrary about the doctrine of eternal punishment; it is merely a case of God respecting our choice, and continuing to us throughout eternity the spiritual condition which we chose to be in while on earth.

To many, this will come as grievous and unwelcome teaching; but we shall be wise not to ignore it, for a great deal of it comes directly from the words of our Lord Himself. A wiser reaction will be to set ourselves to live, as the saints before us have lived, *sub specie aeternitatis*—in the light of eternity. Well did the Psalmist pray, "So teach us to number our days, that we may apply our hearts unto wisdom" (Ps. 90:12). Well did Murray McCheyne paint a setting sun on the dial of his watch, to remind himself how short time is.

We have all eternity to rejoice in victories won for Christ, but only a few brief hours here below in which to win them. All of us need a quickened sense of the shortness of our time, and of the eternal significance of the present moment.

If you cannot make sense of death, you cannot make sense of life either; and no philosophy that will not teach us how to master death is worth two cents to us. At this point the philosophers retire beaten—and the gospel comes into its own. For the mastering of death is, from one point of view, its central theme—the theme which John Owen summed up as *the death of death in the death of Christ*.

Christ's resurrection was no mere temporary resuscitation, as were the raisings of Lazarus, and Jairus' daughter, and the son of the widow of Nain. "Christ being raised from the dead dieth *no more*; death hath *no more dominion* over him . . . he liveth unto God" (Rom. 6:9f.). Again we hear Him say of Himself in Revelation, "I died, and behold *I am alive for evermore*, and I have the keys of Death and Hades."

His rising proclaimed and guaranteed both present forgiveness and justification for His people, as well as their present co-resurrection with Him into newness of spiritual life. This spiritual co-resurrection will be matched when Christ returns by a physical transformation of us if alive, or a re-clothing of us if dead. And that will mean the final destruction of death, as a hostile and destructive intruder into God's world.

Meanwhile, the dread of physical death, which sprang from the sense that death was the door into suffering and judgment (Heb. 2:15), has for the Christian been abolished; death's sting has been drawn through the knowledge that one's sins are forgiven and that "neither death, nor life, ... nor things to come ... nor any other creature, shall be able to separate us from the love of God, which is in Christ Jesus our Lord" (Rom. 8:38f).

Physical death is now no more than "sleep" (*i.e.*, rest and refreshment, Rev. 14:13; not unconsciousness) in Jesus. It is a sleep brought on by Christ's coming to receive to Himself those for whom He has been preparing a place. Fellowship with Christ, once begun here on earth, never ends: through death, through the "intermediate" state between death and resurrection, and forever after, Christ is with His people, and that is life eternal.

Thus He verifies His promise, proclaimed to Martha as she mourned for Lazarus: "I am the resurrection and the life; he who believes in me, though he die, yet shall he live, and whoever lives and believes in me shall never die" (John 11:25f.).

Death is conquered.

Chapter 2

# *BEYOND THE DIVIDE*

By John R. W. Stott

> *But you have come to Mount Zion and to the city of the living God, the heavenly Jerusalem, and to innumerable angels in festal gathering, and to the assembly of the first-born who are enrolled in heaven, and to a judge who is God of all, and to the spirits of just men made perfect, and to Jesus, the mediator of a new covenant, and to the sprinkled blood that speaks more graciously than the blood of Abel.* (Heb. 12:22–24)

Death is hard to define; dictionaries content themselves by saying that it is a cessation of life. In biblical thought death consists of the separation of the soul from the body. At death the body ceases to be the home of the human spirit, and so begins to decay or "return to the dust." But the soul or spirit survives this crisis and lives on in a disembodied condition until the day of resurrection when Christ returns. For this reason the period between death and resurrection is called by theologians "the intermediate state"—not because it is a third alternative, intermediate between heaven

## Beyond the Divide 23

and hell, but because it is a temporary state, intermediate between death and the resurrection.

These "spirits," we believe, are conscious and joyful in the presence of Christ. Nevertheless, their condition is temporary because it is disembodied. They are spirits waiting to be "clothed upon" with a new body, or "body of glory."

The company of the dead to whom we are said to have come consists of the spirits of "just" or "righteous" people. Does this mean that they have got to heaven because of their own righteousness? No, indeed not. The "just" in New Testament language are the "justified," that is, those who have been accepted by God because they are in Christ. They are not those who have made themselves righteous by their own works, but those who have received the righteousness of God as a gift, through faith in Christ. In the language of this Epistle the "just" are those who have fled for refuge to Jesus Christ (6:18), have been sprinkled with His blood (v. 24), whose sins, according to the terms of the New Covenant mediated by Jesus, God will remember no more and who, because God has accepted them in Christ, are striving for holiness without which no man shall see the Lord (v. 14).

They were "just" or "justified" while still on earth. They became "perfected" when they died and went to heaven. This is an important distinction. It shows that to be justified is not to be perfected. The Christian as a justified sinner has been accepted by God, but God's plan of redemption has not yet been completed. The Christian has been redeemed from the guilt and slavery of sin, but he still has an unredeemed body and lives in an unredeemed society. Sin is both within and around him. He is "justified," but not "perfected." It is death which finally delivers the Christian from all sin, because then he leaves behind him for ever both his old body to which the fallen nature belongs, and the sin-stained, sin-spoiled world as well.

If we grasp this, there will be no room for some popular superstitions:

(a) *There is no room for the pitiful doctrine of purgatory.* The Christian dead are "just men made perfect." They may progress in the knowledge of God, as they spend eternity exploring and worshipping His perfections, but there is no room for progress in holiness, since they are already "made perfect." Still less is there any room for the enduring of temporal punishment to expiate their venal sins.

(b) *There is no room for prayers for the dead.* Scripture says that such are "just men made perfect." Why should we pray that God will give them light, peace and rest if we know that He has given to them all these and more, namely perfection?

Christian people are said in verse 22 to have "come to ... the spirits of just men made perfect." There is no biblical warrant for inviting the dead to come to us; it is we who have come to them!

The Christian's attitude to spiritualistic activities is not necessarily to deny their validity, but to forbid their practice. No doubt some spiritualistic phenomena are fraudulent, and others may be explained by telepathy, thought transference or impersonation by evil spirits, but there is no need for Christians to assert that all spiritualistic claims are nonsense. If they were, why would the Scriptures forbid them?

This is not to erect between us and the Christian dead an impenetrable barrier. Although we are forbidden to communicate with them through a medium, we are encouraged to believe that they are watching us. We are said to be "compassed about with a great cloud of witnesses" (v. 1). The holy dead are like low-lying clouds enveloping us and like the serried ranks of spectators at an athletic contest. To remember the spectators will inspire us to run with perseverance.

More than that. Although we must not try to get them to come to us, we can come to them. Indeed, if we are Christians, we have already come to them! When we become Christians we "come to Mount Zion," the dwelling place of God and of the people of God, angels and archangels, the Church militant and triumphant. The redeemed Church of Jesus Christ is one, and death does not destroy its unity. True, it has two sections (the living and the dead); yet it is not two churches but one. It remains a single community, composed of the living and the dead. This is what is meant by the "communion of saints," namely that God has "knit together His elect in one communion and fellowship." It is not a conscious communion, a "mystic sweet communion with those whose rest is won," but rather a recognition that in Christ even death can not separate us.

In conclusion, there are two lessons about the Christian dead which seem to stand out in this study:

(a) *They are perfected.* Although they are temporarily disembodied spirits, they are perfected and lack nothing necessary to moral perfection. It would be foolish therefore to worry about them or pray for them as if their condition were unsatisfactory. It would also be selfish, even if it were possible, to attempt to drag them back to contact with this sinful world.

(b) *We have come to them.* We are not to think of them as entirely sundered from us. We may speak of them as having gone from us, but we can also say that we have come to them. Our life is hid with Christ in God, for we are seated with Christ in heavenly places, where they are too. We can especially realize this when we come to worship, because it is then that the thick curtains of sense and space are lifted and we seem to step into eternity. We offer our worship "with angels and archangels and with all the company of heaven." Such an awareness will add a new dimension to our Christian worship.

Chapter 3

# DEATH: JESUS MADE IT ALL DIFFERENT

By Gordon Chilvers

When Jesus arose from the dead, death was radically changed for the Christian. A careful study of the New Testament's pictures of death shows the magnitude of this particular transformation and gives us a most heartening view of the future.

First of all, for the Christian death is a sleep. The word for sleep, *koimaomai*, is used 18 times in the New Testament, and 14 of these refer to the sleep of death. After Lazarus had died Jesus said, "Our friend Lazarus sleepeth; but I go, that I may awake him out of sleep." When Stephen had given his convicting testimony to the Jews, they stoned him to death. But we read, "he fell asleep" (Acts 7:60). And Paul speaks of the dead as those who "sleep in Jesus" (I Thess. 4:14).

What a blessing sleep can be! It is the fitting sequel to labor. The sleep of death brings rest to those who have labored here on earth. "Blessed are the dead which die in the Lord from henceforth: Yea, saith the Spirit, that they may rest from their labors; and their works do follow them" (Rev.

14:13). Sleep is an experience from which we awake rested and refreshed, ready for the day's work. And from death we awake ready to live in a new world. Life has its pain and problems, but sleep brings relief from all pain and suffering. So when death comes it ends all the pain and suffering that we have had to endure on earth.

The pagans also spoke of death as a sleep, however. But how different is the Christian from the pagan thought! Catullus wrote: "When once our brief light sets, there is one perpetual night through which we must sleep." Theocritus wrote: "There is hope for those who are alive, but those who have died are without hope." And this grim epitaph was carved on some tombstones: "I was not; I became; I am not; I care not."

To Christians sleep in death means to awake in resurrection. We know that we shall live again. Jesus assured us, "Because I live, ye shall live also" (John 14:19). When the Christian dies we do not write the words, "the end"; we write, "to be continued," and turn over the page. As Luther has said, the righteous dead will sleep until the Lord comes to knock on the grave and bid them wake up.

When Lazarus died, his sleep was undisturbed by any noise until the Lord shouted, "Lazarus, come forth. And he that was dead came forth, bound hand and foot with graveclothes: and his face was bound about with a napkin" (John 11:43, 44). He had responded to his name. So we shall sleep until the hour "when the dead shall hear the voice of the Son of God: and they that hear shall live" (John 5:25).

A second picture of death in the New Testament is Paul's image of departure (*analusis*). He writes

## Death: Jesus Made It All Different 29

in II Timothy 4:6, "For I am now ready to be offered, and the time of my departure is at hand."

There are many uses of this word in secular Greek, each of which tells us something of what death means to a Christian. They are exemplified in the life of Paul. One picture is that of the ox that is loosed from the cart, or the plough when the day's work is finished. Paul knew toil as few other men have ever known it. He described one part of his life as being "in labors more abundant" (II Cor. 11:23). When death came to him it would mean an end to labor. He would then lay down his burden for ever and enjoy the rest of God.

Another picture is that of a ship which has been tied up to a dirty dock, but is soon to set sail. The anchor is pulled up and the mooring ropes that have held the ship to the shore have been loosed (the same word). The sails are unfurled and filled with a favorable breeze. It is soon heading for the happy shore where home is. The seas and their perils were most familiar to Paul. Often he had been shipwrecked, and had once spent a night and a day adrift on the deep. Soon he was to launch out across a sea he had never sailed before. But it was one on which he had no fear of being wrecked; he was sure to gain his haven.

"Departure" takes on another shade of meaning in the picture of a soldier striking camp. He loosens the ropes that hold the tent in place, pulls up the tent pins and goes on his journey. William Barclay reminds us of what happened in the terrible days of World War II when the Royal Air Force stood between England and destruction, and the lives of its pilots were being sacrificially spent. The people never spoke of a pilot as having been killed. They always referred to him as having been "posted to another station."

Paul was well acquainted with the moving of tents, for he was a tentmaker by trade. Soon he would be striking his tent for the last time. Then he would make his most important journey, the one that leads to the city of God. As he wrote to the Philippian church (1:23), "I am in a strait betwixt two, having a desire to depart, and to be with Christ; which is far better."

When the fetters that hold a man in prison are struck off and he is loosed, we get another picture of what "departure" can mean. Paul knew it. He was bound with fetters many times and wrote several of his epistles while chained to a Roman guard. But when death came he would be free from his bonds forever—spiritual as well as physical.

Paul's life is illustrative of one further meaning of "departure." It is seen in the picture of someone solving a problem. When the answer has been found the problem is no longer fixed—it is loosed from its difficulty. There was a multitude of problems facing Paul throughout his life. Some were personal, others were in connection with the churches. But when death came he would know as he was known (I Cor. 13:12) and all his problems would be solved at once.

But the New Testament not only pictures death as sleep or as a departure. It is also seen as an *exodus*. Peter says in his second epistle (1:15): "I will endeavor that ye may be able after my decease to have these things always in remembrance." In King James' version the word translated "decease" is also used of Christ's death. Moses and Elijah "appeared in glory, and spake of his decease which he should accomplish at Jerusalem" (Luke 9:31).

## Death: Jesus Made It All Different 31

In the only other passage in which the word is used, it refers to the children of Israel leaving Egypt. "By faith Joseph, when he died, made mention of the departing of the children of Israel; and gave commandment concerning his bones" (Heb. 11:22).

This is an excellent picture of what death meant to Peter and should mean to us. The children of Israel had known bitter bondage for many years. The Egyptians had used them as slaves and made them build Pharaoh's treasure cities from their own resources.

But with their exodus from Egypt all this was finished. They were free from their taskmasters with the cruel whips. They were on their way to God's inheritance for them, "a land flowing with milk and honey." What a contrast!

Peter's exodus would be just such a great change for him. He had labored hard and long for the Lord. He had endured misunderstandings and imprisonments. Persecution would at last bring about his exodus.

Then he would go out that he might enter into the home that Christ had spoken of. Death was not the end. He was not going out into the dark, but into the light. As Quinton Hogg says: "Death is not only an exodus, it is also an entrance; while we stand by the bedside and say, 'He is gone,' they on the other side are welcoming him with unspeakable joy."

The traveler to Italy often enters the Mount Cevis tunnel with foreboding. The world and its light are shut out. He feels the stifling gloom and he can be almost terrified by a horror of helplessness. But all the time he is moving, and when he emerges it is into the Italian air. Then there is the dazzling sunshine. There are the snowy peaks on either side, uplifted into the stainless blue. We are through the darkness of death and we enter into a better country.

That great British writer Charles Kingsley lay dying in his room. In another room his wife was dangerously ill and was not expected to recover. This was their first separation in a married life of unclouded love and confidence. She sent him a message one day, to ask if he thought it cowardly for a poor soul to tremble before the mystery of that unknown world. "Not cowardly," was the response, "but remember it is not darkness we are going to, for God is light; not loneliness, for Christ is with us."

Except for those who are alive when Jesus returns, we must all face death. Yet it need hold no terrors for us. Jesus has conquered death and risen from the tomb. For us, death is a sleep to awake in eternal happiness, a departure from this world to be with Christ, an exodus from earth with its trials to go to our eternal home.

Chapter 4

## *THE LAST SAY*

By Miriam G. Moran

It was a bright, crisp day in late November. As we entered the little New England town a carillon was playing Christmas carols.

God rest ye merry, gentlemen,
Let nothing you dismay.
Remember Christ our Savior
Was born on Christmas day,
To save us all from Satan's power
When we were gone astray.

O tidings of comfort and joy!

We had to drive around town a bit before we found what we were looking for—the Roswell funeral home. My husband's grandfather had died, and we had come for the funeral.

I had met him only once. He and his oldest daughter lived alone in the old homestead nearby. We had visited them for two days just the summer before. I remember he shuffled almost sprightly out to our car—a short little man, dressed in blue jeans and a flannel shirt, with the whitest hair I had ever seen.

"Well, Baby Allen!" he said to my husband, and glanced mischievously at me. (He would always use that diminutive to distinguish grandson from son.) "You don't look like your father any more than you ever did. But come on in." His voice was raspy, and he coughed as he spoke.

The old home was sparsely furnished, but clean. And in the living room, beside his chair, was the box of paperback Westerns my husband had told me about. He sat down and tried to light his pipe, but his hands trembled so that it took him awhile. When he had finally succeeded, he leaned back and smiled.

"Been doin' a little readin'," he said, as he noticed me eyeing the box of worn books. "Ever read Zane Grey?"

But now Grandpa was dead. And his would be my first funeral.

Everything was hushed as we entered the funeral home. The air was laden with the mingled aroma of cigarettes, perfume, and the scent of flowers. In another little room lay the coffin, with the children and grandchildren standing by. We joined them, and I had my first look at Death.

It wasn't Grandpa. The trembling hands were still. The eyes which had smiled at us were closed. And the chest which had so often been racked by cough just stayed there, stationary, as still as the hand resting upon it. His daughter, weeping, touched the hand. But there was no response.

Death. Who could have the audacity to call it beautiful? Or even natural? It was a horrible mockery, and outrage. It shouldn't *be*.

Frustrated, I followed my husband to our seats in the family section.

"Let not your hearts be troubled," the minister began in doleful tones. I couldn't see the minister. He was in another room, and his voice was coming over an intercom system. "I go to prepare a place for you. And if I go to prepare a place for you, I will come again, and receive you unto myself; that where I am, there you may be also."

It was nice to think of Grandpa being in heaven. But what about Death? This horrible wrenching of soul from body? This robbery which takes the person but leaves his body as a cruel reminder to us of the one we have lost?

Is that really natural? Beautiful? Did God intend it this way? Is it the best He can do—simply to intercept the spirit and take it to heaven? Can't anybody do anything about Death itself? Will it always have the last say?

The funeral service finally ended, and we were back out in the clear November air and bright sunshine.

"Good Christian men, rejoice!" the carillon was playing. "Now ye need not fear the grave: Jesus Christ was born to save."

Jesus Christ was born to save.

We drove in silence to the cemetery. The rectangular grave was all ready, but not even the carpet of fake grass could disguise the mound of dirt beside it. The minister turned his overcoat collar up around his neck and began dutifully to read some more.

"If in this life only we have hope in Christ, we are of all men most miserable. But now is Christ risen from the dead, and is become the first fruits of them that slept. . . . Then cometh the end, when he shall have delivered up the kingdom to God, even the Father. For he must reign, till he hath put all enemies under his feet. *The last enemy that shall be destroyed is Death. . . ."*

Death . . . will be destroyed. Christ will do it.

"Christ was born for this! Christ was born for this!"

Suddenly it all telescoped. He is a complete Savior. He is Victor. He will have the last say.

The Apostle John wrote to his beloved children, from whom Death would soon be taking him, "The Son of God appeared for the very purpose of *undoing* the devil's work."

Christmas marks the beginning of that undoing.

"Earth to earth, ashes to ashes, dust to dust," the minister intoned. Death had won this round. Grandpa had become yet another of his victims.

But there will be another round. And in that round the conqueror will be Life, the One whom to know is Life Eternal. Death will be swallowed up in victory. And there shall be no more death, neither sorrow, nor crying.

## Chapter 5

# *SORROW WITH HOPE*

### By Donald Grey Barnhouse

NO ONE who has traveled in India can ever forget the beating of the death drums. The first time I heard them was in the city of Madura, near the tip of India. We had been out all day in the bustle of the city and had noticed them only occasionally; the noises of the busy city had almost stifled them. But as darkness came on, those noises faded out and that other, sinister noise suddenly became dominant, like the pulse in the ears of a man in fever. Louder and louder it came. Persistently it struck, hammering through the dark. Beating, beating drums. Hopelessness itself. On and on it went, until the mind seemed almost drugged. It is India itself. India is death. Souls in the dark. This is Satan's tune of death.

We don't have the noise of drums in our sophisticated Western lands. But let us not be deceived. Unbelievers may have stolen a bit of perfume from Christianity to stifle the odor of death, but the hopelessness is still there. They, just as much as the benighted souls in India, are among those "who have no hope."

By contrast, the Christian is full of hope. Death strikes his family circle, too. A mother or father succumbs to illness and is gone. A child is taken from the parents who have watched over the little life so earnestly. A grim accident cuts off a husband or wife. And the Christian who is left behind sorrows. The Lord did not dehumanize us when we were born again. In fact, the springs of human love run more deeply in those who have been to the cross of Calvary to have their love purified. But our sorrow is tempered by hope.

Our Heavenly Father knows our sorrow, He knows our tears, He cares for us. For this reason He has given us a special revelation concerning the death of our loved ones: "But I would not have you to be ignorant, brethren, concerning them who are asleep, that ye sorrow not, even as others which have no hope. For if we believe that Jesus died and rose again, even so them also which sleep in Jesus will God bring with him" (I Thess. 4:13, 14).

Significantly, the text of this truth is found in the earliest book of the New Testament. The early Church had grown up around the thought of the empty tomb of the Lord Jesus Christ. As they met to break bread and drink the cup of communion, Calvary with all its grim shadows was behind them, the glorious return of the Lord before them. But suddenly death reached into the circle of those early Christians, and there was a funeral. We do not know who was the first Christian to die. Stephen was the first martyr, but undoubtedly there were many many deaths among believers before his.

So, there arose in the hearts of these young Christians doubts and questionings concerning their loved ones. Yesterday they had all been together in the warmth of life and the glow of expectancy of the Lord's return. Now they were forced to bury a human body, recently vibrant with life, and to realize anew that this body was made of dust and would return to dust. Jesus Christ had borne the penalty of their spiritual death, yet the shadow of it was still upon their bodies and full redemption would not be complete until some far distant day. Thus, the revelation of God concerning death was given to them.

Oh, thank God that we are on His side of the frontier of death! The pulsing of His blood as it slipped out of His body on Calvary stilled for us forever the beat of the death drums. Jesus Christ has died. Jesus Christ will come again and when He comes He will bring with Him all of the Christian dead. If you as a Christian know this fact, it will give hope to your sorrow when death enters your home.

Where are the Christian dead at the present moment?

Some have said that they are unconscious. But our text speaks of those who are asleep, and it can be affirmed that not one line in the Bible teaches that the Christian dead—or any other dead—are in a state of unconsciousness. It is true that a body in death closely resembles sleep and so the image of sleep was adopted to picture death. But the spirit of man has never slept and will not be unconscious, even for a moment. "Therefore, we are always confident, knowing that, while we are at home in the body we are absent from the Lord ... we are confident, I say, and willing rather to be absent from the body to be present with the Lord" (II Cor. 5:6, 8).

When absence from the body begins, then begins

presence with the Lord. Paul said as much when he wrote to the Philippian church. He was speaking of his eager desire to go to heaven, to be where Christ was. But the Lord showed him there was a great work yet to be done on earth and Paul was willing to do it: "For to me to live is Christ, but to die is gain. . . . But what I shall choose, I do not know, because I am in a strait betwixt two, having a desire to depart and be with Christ; which is far better. Nevertheless to abide in the flesh is more needful to you" (Phil. 1:21-24).

If there had been a long period of soul-sleep between death and the resurrection, or some period of self-purgation, Paul would have said, "Don't let me die now; let me stay on in life as long as I can be of some use; I don't want to go to a state of unconsciousness." But, knowing the truth of God, he forever swept aside the false teachings about life after death. To depart is to be *with* Christ, and that is far better than life *in* Christ which is, of course, better than unconsciousness, better than any purgatory or suffering. "I would not have you to be ignorant," says the Lord, "that you sorrow not, even as others which have no hope, for if we believe that Jesus died and rose again, even so them also which sleep in Jesus, God will bring with Him."

The resurrection is two-directional. It is from heaven and from the earth. The bodies of the Christian dead have gone to sleep in the dust of the earth; they will rise up when Christ returns. Their spirits and souls have gone to heaven, in full consciousness, to be with the Lord; these God will bring with Christ when He comes. So the souls from heaven and the bodies from earth will be forever joined at the coming of the Lord.

## Sorrow with Hope

As we understand this, we are able to sorrow *with hope* when death enters the circle of our friends and loved ones. The separation is but for a time. Our loved ones have gone on to something far better. In blessed consciousness of the life which is Christ, they wait in heaven for the end of this present age. Then He, Christ, will rise from the throne of God and will come forth from heaven to receive us to Himself.

"Let not your heart be troubled," He says. "You believe in God, believe also in Me. In My Father's house are many mansions; if it were not so, I would have told you. I go to prepare a place for you. And if I go and prepare a place for you, I will come again, and receive you unto Myself, that where I am, there you may be also" (John 14:1–3).

Chapter 6

# *THE ONES WHO ARE LEFT*

By Elisabeth Elliot

"It's gone." I could see the yellow-spoked wheel of the spare tire, perched on the back of a 1934 Plymouth, disappear over the hilltop. The car in which I might have got a ride home from elementary school on this rainy day had gone and I was left.

"It's gone." The trainman stood at the only lighted gate in Penn Station. The train had gone, leaving me behind to figure out how on earth I was to make a speaking engagement on Long Island in an hour and a half.

We've all experienced the desolation of being left in one way or another. And sooner or later many of us experience the greatest desolation of all: he's gone. The one who made life what it was for us, who was, in fact, our life.

And we were not ready. Not really prepared at all. We felt, when the fact stared us in the face, "No. Not yet." For however bravely we may have looked at the possibilities (if we had any warning at all), however calmly we may have talked about them with the one who was about to die (and I had a chance to talk about the high risks with my first husband, and about the human hopelessness of his situation with my second), we are caught short. If we had another week, perhaps, to brace ourselves. A few more days to say what we wanted to say, to do or undo some things, wouldn't it have been better, easier?

But silent, swift, and implacable the Scythe has swept by, and he is gone, and we are left. We stand bewildered on the sidewalk, on the station platform. Yet, most strangely, that stunning snatching away has changed nothing very much. There is the sunlight lying in patches on the familiar carpet just as it did yesterday. The same dishes stand in the rack to be put away as usual, his razor and comb are on the shelf, his shoes in the closet (O the shoes! molded in the always recognizable shape of his feet). The mail comes, the phone rings, Wednesday gives way to Thursday and this week to next week, and you have to keep getting up in the morning ("Life must go on, I forget just why," wrote Edna St. Vincent Millay) and combing your hair (for whom, now?), eating breakfast (remember to get out only one egg now, not three), making the bed (who cares?). You have to meet people who most fervently wish they could pass by on the other side so as not to have to think of something to say. You have to be understanding with *their* attempts to be understanding, and when they nervously try to steer you away from the one topic you want so desperately to talk about you have to allow yourself to be steered away—for their sakes. You resist the temptation, when they say he's "passed away," to say "No, he's *dead*, you know."

After a few months you've learned those initial lessons. You begin to say "I" instead of "we" and people have sent their cards and flowers and said the things they ought to say and their lives are going on and so, astonishingly, is yours and you've "adjusted" to some of the differences—as if that little mechanical word, a mere tinkering with your routines and emotions, covers the ascent from the pit.

I speak of the "ascent." I am convinced that every death, of whatever kind, through which we are called to go, must lead to a resurrection. This is the core of Christian faith. Death is the end of every life and leads to resurrection, the beginning of every new one. It is a progression, a proper progression, the way things were meant to be, the necessary means of ongoing life. It is supremely important that every bereaved person be helped to see this. The death of the beloved was the beloved's own death, "a very private personal matter," Gert Behanna says, "and nobody should ever dare to try to get in on the act." But the death of the beloved is also the lover's death, for it means, in a different but perhaps equally fearsome way, a going through the Valley of the Shadow.

I can think of six simple things that have helped me through this valley and that help me now.

First, I try to be still and know that He is God. That advice comes from Psalm 46, which begins by describing the sort of trouble from which God is our refuge—the earth's changing, or "giving way" as the Jerusalem Bible puts it, the mountains shaking, the waters roaring and foaming, nations raging, kingdoms tottering, the earth melting. None of these cataclysms seems an exaggeration of what happens when somebody dies. The things that seemed most dependable have given way altogether. The whole world has a different look and

## The Ones Who Are Left

you find it hard to get your bearings. Shadows can be very confusing. But in both psalms we are reminded of one rock-solid fact that nothing can change: Thou art with me. The Lord of Hosts is with us, the God of Jacob is our refuge. We feel that we are alone, yet we are not alone. Not for one moment has He left us alone. He is the one who has "wrought desolations," to be sure. He makes wars cease, breaks bows, shatters spears, burns chariots (breaks hearts, shatters lives?), but in the midst of all this hullabaloo we are commanded, *"Be still."* Be still and know.

Stillness is something the bereaved may feel they have entirely too much of. But if they will use that stillness to take a long look at Christ, to listen attentively to his voice, they will get their bearings.

There are several ways of looking and listening that help us avoid being dangerously at the mercy of our (heaven forfend!) "gut-level" feelings. Bible reading and prayer are the obvious ones. Taking yourself by the scruff of the neck and setting aside a definite time in a definite place for deliberately looking at what God has said and listening to what he may have to say to you today is a good exercise. And if such exercises are seen as an obligation, they have the same power other obligations—cooking a meal, cleaning a bathroom, vacuuming a rug—have to save us from ourselves.

Another means of grace is repeating the creed. Here is a list of objective facts that have not been in the smallest detail altered by what has happened to us. Far from it. Not only have they not been altered; they do actually alter what has happened—alter our whole understanding of human life and death, lift it to another plane. We can go through the list and contemplate our situation in the light of each tremendous truth. It is simply amazing how different my situation can appear as a result of this discipline.

The second thing I try to do is to give thanks. I cannot thank God for the murder of one or the excruciating disintegration of another, but I can thank God for the promise of his presence. I can thank him that he is still in charge, in the face of life's worst terrors, and that "this slight momentary affliction is preparing for us [not 'us for'] an eternal weight of glory beyond all comparison, because we look not to the things that are seen but to the things that are unseen." I'm back to the creed again and the things unseen that are listed there, standing solidly (yes, solidly, incredible as it seems) against things seen (the fact of death, my own loneliness, this empty room). And I am lifted up by the promise of that "weight" of glory, so far greater than the weight of sorrow that at times seems to grind me like a millstone. This promise enables me to give thanks.

Then I try to refuse self-pity. I know of nothing more paralyzing, more deadly, than self-pity. It is a death that has no resurrection, a sink-hole from which no rescuing hand can drag you because you have chosen to sink. But it must be refused. In order to refuse it, of course, I must recognize it for what it is. Amy Carmichael, in her sword-thrust of a book, *If*, wrote, "If I make much of anything appointed, magnify it secretly to myself or insidiously to others, then I know nothing of Calvary love." That's a good definition of self-pity—making much of the "appointed," magnifying it, dwelling on one's own losses, looking with envy on those who appear to be more fortunate then oneself, asking "why me, Lord?" (remembering the "weight of glory" ought to be a sufficient answer to that question). It is one thing to call a spade a spade, to acknowledge that this thing is indeed suffering. It's no use telling yourself it's nothing. When Paul called it a "slight" affliction he meant it only by comparison with the glory. But it's another thing to regard one's own suffering as uncommon, or disproportionate, or undeserved. What have "deserts" got to do with anything? We are all under the Mercy, and Christ knows the precise weight and proportion of our sufferings—*he bore them*. He carried our sorrows. He suffered, wrote George Macdonald, not that we might not suffer, but that our sufferings might be like his. To hell, then, with self-pity.

The next thing to do is to accept my loneliness. When God takes a loved person from my life it is in order to call me, in a new way, to himself. It is therefore a vocation. It is in this sphere, for now, anyway, that I am to learn of him. Every stage on the pilgrimage is a chance to know him, to be brought to him. Loneliness is a stage (and, thank God, only a stage) when we are terribly aware of our own helplessness. It "opens the gates of my soul," wrote Katherine Mansfield, "and lets the wild beasts stream howling through." We may accept this, thankful that it brings us to the Very Present Help.

The acceptance of loneliness can be followed immediately by the offering of it up to God. Something mysterious and miraculous transpires as soon as something is held up in our hands as a gift. He takes it from us, as Jesus took the little lunch when five thousand people were hungry. He gives thanks for it and then, breaking it, transforms it for the good of others. Loneliness looks pretty paltry as a gift to offer to God—but then when you come to think of it so does anything else we might offer. It needs transforming. Others looking at it would say exactly what the disciples said, "What's the good of that with such a crowd?" But it was none of their business what use the Son of God would make of it. And it is none of ours. It is ours only to give it.

The last of the helps I have found is to do something for somebody else. There is nothing like definite, overt action to overcome the inertia of grief. The appearance of Joseph of Arimathea to take away the body of Jesus must have greatly heartened the other disciples, so prostrate with their own grief that they had probably not thought of doing anything at all. Nicodemus, too, thought of something he could do—he brought a mixture of myrrh and aloes—and the women who had come with Jesus from Galilee went off to prepare spices and ointments. This clear-cut action lifted them out of themselves. That is what we need in a time of crisis. An old piece of wisdom is "Doe the next thynge." Most of us have someone who needs us. If we haven't, we can find someone. Instead of praying only for the strength we ourselves need to survive, this day or this hour, how about praying for some to give away? How about trusting God to fulfill his own promise, "My strength is made perfect in weakness"? Where else is his strength more perfectly manifested than in a human being who, well knowing his own weakness, lays hold by faith on the Strong Son of God, Immortal Love?

It is here that a great spiritual principle goes into operation. Isaiah 58:10–12 says, "If you pour yourself out for the hungry and satisfy the desire of the afflicted, then shall your light rise in the darkness and your gloom be as the noonday. And the Lord will guide you continually and satisfy your desire with good things, and make your bones strong; and you shall be like a watered garden, like a spring of water, whose waters fail not, and ... you shall be called a repairer of the breach, the restorer of streets to dwell in [or, in another translation, 'paths leading home']."

The condition on which all these wonderful gifts (light, guidance, satisfaction, strength, refreshment to others) rests is an unexpected one—unexpected, that is, if we are accustomed to think in material instead of in spiritual terms. The condition is not that one solve his own problems first. He need not "get it together." The condition is simply "if you pour yourself out."

Countless others have found this to work. St. Francis of Assisi put the principle into other words in his great prayer, "Lord, make me an instrument of thy peace. Where there is darkness let me sow light, where there is sadness, joy. . . . Grant that I may not so much seek to be consoled as to console. . . . For it is in giving that we receive; it is in pardoning that we are pardoned; it is in dying that we are born to eternal life." The words of this prayer were like a light to me in the nights of my husband's last illness, and I wondered then at the marvel of a man's prayer being answered (was I the millionth to be blessed by it?) some seven hundred years after he had prayed it. St. Francis was most certainly during those nights in 1973 an instrument of God's peace.

Perhaps it is peace, of all God's earthly gifts, that in our extremity we long for most. A priest told me of a terminally ill woman who asked him each time he came to visit only to pray, "The peace of God which passeth all understanding keep your hearts and minds through Christ Jesus."

I have often prayed, in thinking of the many bereaved, the words of the beautiful hymn "Sun of my Soul":

> Be every mourner's sleep tonight
> Like infant slumbers, pure and bright.

There they are—six things that, if done in faith, can be the way to resurrection: be still and know, give thanks, refuse self-pity, accept the loneliness, offer it to God, turn your energies toward the satisfaction not of your own needs but of others'. And there will be no calculating the extent to which

> From the ground there blossoms red Life that shall endless be.

Chapter 7

# A TIME TO BE BORN AND A TIME TO DIE

By David H. Freeman

The christian needs to be a defender of the right to life, and the right to die. Both rights are threatened today. In the United States alone the unborn are being legally killed at the rate of more than 900,000 a year. Proposals to make legal the killing of the newly born have already been made, and serious consideration is being given to the destruction of the retarded, the insane, the old, and the dying.

Human life—whether that of a zygote, a fetus, a newly born infant, a child, a mature adult, or an old man—is regarded as having no intrinsic value. Instead, it is considered on a par with every other living organism. What rights or values are to be assigned to human life is a question for man and man alone to decide. Who is to be born, who is to live, and who is to die, are held to be matters of public policy, legal—not moral—concerns.

Never before has there been greater need of witness to the truth that human life owes its origin and value to its Creator. Man is set apart by his having been made in the image and likeness of

God. The command "Thou shalt not kill" does not confer sanctity and inviolability on human life; God's command simply demands the recognition of what is there already. Our thoughts, words, deeds ought to acknowledge human life as intrinsically valuable because God made man so. Man's right to live at any age is not given to him by his mother, nor by both parents, nor by the state, nor by society as such. His right to life and the value of his life were given to him by God at his very creation.

All human life has a quality, a God-given quality, a quality which distinguishes it from the life of every other organism. Man may not be distinguished biochemically; he, too, is dust, but he is distinct "theologically"; he is precious in the eyes of God.

God is a God of the living. Those who have passed from darkness into light, from death into life, are called to cry out in protest in defense of life.

The right to live, however, needs to be balanced by the right to die. "There is a time to be born and a time to die," the Preacher said. Our right to die, too, is under attack by the well-meant misuse of medical knowledge, surgical skill, and technology.

The command "Thou shalt not kill" precludes a Christian from engaging in or assisting in the direct killing of another human no matter how noble the motive and no matter what the circumstances. A Christian may never intend the death of the innocent. He can never be the willing agent, the instrument, the immediate cause of the death of what is, was, or will become a human being.

A distinction is frequently drawn between active euthanasia and passive euthanasia. However, if by "active euthanasia" one understands the intentional, active taking or ending of human life where mercy is the motive, and if by "passive euthanasia" one understands the withholding of medical support, thereby allowing the disease or physical condition to kill the patient, it is confusing to use the term "euthanasia" in both instances. In the former case one human being is the *cause* of the death of another, in the latter a person's *own* disease or physical condition is responsible for his death. Failure to give a particular medicine, to use a particular drug, to perform surgery, to utilize radiation, to undergo dialysis, to plug into a heart and lung machine, to receive a transplant, or even to give intravenous feeding may be the occasion, but it is not the cause of death. The cause is the disease, the physical condition of the dying.

Contrary to much opinion, I do not believe that the Scriptures place us under a moral obligation to prolong human life simply because it is technically possible to do so. Jacob, for instance, quietly, after calling his sons together, "gathered up his feet into the bed, and yielded up the ghost, and was gathered unto his people." In all probability the Egyptian physicians possessed medication which could have prolonged Jacob's life for days or possibly weeks. Our age is prone to the technological fallacy: whatever is technologically possible must necessarily be done, and whatever is at our disposal must be used.

Technology frequently is employed to prolong human life beyond the point where the patient can ever again function in a manner enabling him to serve God. Human life is to be prolonged, when possible, when there is a reasonable expectation that the patient will recover sufficiently to enable him to accomplish whatever task God has for him. Man's life belongs to God and man's end is to glorify and to enjoy him forever. When a Christian's physical condition makes such service no longer possible on earth, he has the *right* to continue to glorify and to enjoy God in heaven. His earthly task is over.

A distinction is sometimes made between the use of ordinary versus extraordinary means of prolonging life, and it is held that whereas ordinary means must be used, there is no obligation to use extraordinary means. This distinction is, however, in my opinion, so extremely relative that it is no longer serviceable. For what is extraordinary when first introduced may with use become quite ordinary. And in extreme cases, what would usually be quite ordinary—for example, the use of antibiotics or intravenous feeding—may become quite extraordinary.

The realization that God has no further task, that in his providence our life work is at an end, may in itself be a sufficient reason to allow the transition from this world to the next. Such a passing can be made as comfortable as possible. Pain, both physical and mental, has its proper function. It serves as a warning, reminds us of our finitude, and may prepare us for death. But beyond a certain point pain can become unbearable torture. Drugs are available and may even be given when their use may have the secondary effect of hastening or resulting in the end. The sole intent, however, must be the alleviating of suffering and never the death of the patient.

The patient's right to die, not simply his subjective feelings and desires, are to be respected. However, in the case of the non-Christian, every effort should be made to reach him with the gospel. The conspiracy of silence, the practice of deception which often surrounds the dying, must be broken.

## A Time to be Born and a Time to Die 55

For the unbeliever there awaits an eternity of separation from God, a suffering far worse than anything here imaginable. Christian physicians and nurses, Christian friends and relatives, Christian pastors and workers should spend as much time as is possible with the dying, pointing them to the way of victory over death. There will be no other chance.

But the believer, by preparing for and dying his own death in a Christian way, can make his last act a final witness to others. Preparation for death should begin in the time of health. In each waking moment the Christian ought to realize that God is his Father, heaven is home, that every day is one day nearer. He ought to long for the time when with the family of God he will stand before God's throne. With such an attitude death can be approached without depression, without anger, and without fear, rather with courage, peace, and even joy. There will of course be sorrow, too, sorrow for the tasks undone, sadness at the separation from what we love here below, but at the same time there can be an exhilarating expectation and a recognition that while we shall be missed, we shall soon miss nothing of this world. To die is gain!

Our final days and hours provide the opportunity to communicate the good news to our doctors, nurses, friends, and family, not simply verbally—there must be words, too—but nonverbally by reflecting our faith, our hope, and our desire to be with Jesus, even amidst our suffering and pain. Every word, every movement, every bodily expression radiates what we truly believe.

We can show our attitude toward death in time of health by making it clear to our physician and to our family that when our earthly task is over, we wish to claim our right to die, that if we are unable to express our desires, there is to be no artificial prolonging or biological existence. The only life we would prolong is that life which is a part of God's plan for us, a life that includes a God-given task for us to perform. We do not desire death simply to escape pain, and the frailty of old age, but we are ready to leave when our work is done.

Our witness can extend beyond our death if in our will we continue our stewardship by insisting that our burial be free of the wasteful extravagance so frequently surrounding the "American way of death." There is no need for expensive coffins, costly headstones, endless flowers. A pine box, a simple marker, a single bouquet, and a gospel service are all that a Christian should desire. Instead of flowers and costly funeral expenses we can request that money be given to mission causes.

The world is to know that we sorrow not as the ungodly but that the last enemy has been conquered. We know that: "The Lord himself shall descend from heaven with a shout . . . and the dead in Christ shall rise . . . we shall ever be with the Lord. With these words we are to comfort one another."

Chapter 8

# *MERCY-DYING* vs. *MERCY-KILLING*

By Norman Geisler

IN THE controversy surrounding the care of terminally ill patients, a distinction should be made between *taking* a life and *letting* one die. The former may be wrong; whereas the latter in the same situation need not be wrong. For example, to withdraw the medication from a terminal patient and allow him to die naturally need not be a moral wrong. In some cases—where the individual and/or loved ones consent—this may be the most merciful thing to do. Indeed, if an illness is incurable and the individual is being kept alive only by a machine, then pulling the plug may be an act of mercy.

This is not to say that a doctor should give medicine or perform an operation to speed death—that could very well be murder. But this position does imply that mercifully *permitting* the sufferer to die is morally right, whereas *precipitating* his death is not. Medicine should be given to relieve suffering but not to hasten death. If, however, the lack of medicine or machine can lessen suffering by allowing death to occur sooner, then why should one be morally bound to perpetuate the patient's suffering by artificial means? In brief, killing involves *taking* the life of another whereas natural dying does not; it is merely *letting* one die. A man is responsible for the former, but God is responsible for the latter.

The objection that miracles do happen even in supposedly "incurable cases" is sometimes leveled against allowing mercy-dyings. Why not keep the person alive and pray for a miracle? Or, maybe a cure will be discovered by scientists if the individual can be kept alive long enough. In attempting to answer this question it is necessary to point out that one should be kept alive as long as there is any reason for hope (medically or supernaturally) that he can recover to a meaningful human life.

However, when both God and medical science have been given ample opportunity to cure the disease and yet it appears beyond all reasonable doubt that this patient will have little more than a "vegetable" type of existence, then one may conclude that God wants him to die a natural death. The basic moral principle behind this conclusion is that one ought not perpetuate an inhumanity while futilely waiting for a miracle. Hoping for a cure without any assurance it will come while one delays an act of natural mercy does not seem morally justifiable. Waiting without reasonable expectation for grace is not a justifiable basis for refusing to allow mercy to do its work.

There is another overall moral principle at work here. The obligation of humans to perpetuate life does not mean that one should be obligated to perpetuate it if it is no longer a *human* life in any significant sense of that word. As a matter of fact, it is morally wrong to perpetuate an inhumanity. If a monstrously deformed baby dies naturally, it should be considered an act of divine mercy. A doctor should not feel morally obligated to resuscitate a monster or human "vegetable." Just as the moral command is not to take a *human* life, so one's duty is only to perpetuate a *human* life.

The Christian's desire for death (cf. Phil. 1:23) may lead him fearlessly to face death but should never lead him carelessly or selfishly to take his own life. Nor should it lead him to ask another to help him. The Christian should welcome death from God's hand but not force the hand that brings it.

CHAPTER 9

## *A DOCTOR SPEAKS FROM THE NURSING HOME*

By Larry Edwards

AFTER DECADES of being taboo, death is now an in subject in America. *Psychology Today* recently received 30,000 replies to a questionnaire on death, surpassing the previous record of 20,000 replies to a questionnaire on sex. In addition, about 10 percent of the respondees wrote letters describing their feelings about death.

It is important for each of us to understand how we view the process of dying. Often Christians have a good practical theology of "after death," but the dying process itself is something they haven't thought much about.

My own interests in this subject have evolved primarily because of my experience as medical director of two geriatric institutions, where there is a predictable 10-to-20 percent mortality rate. In watching members of the older generation die, I have observed a haunting dilemma.

For many years our way of death was influenced by our Judeo-Christian heritage. The closing chapters of Genesis tell us how Jacob died. After calling his children and grandchildren around him, he gave them his blessing and judgment. "Then he told them, 'Soon I will die. You must bury me with my fathers in the land of Canaan in the cave in the field of Mach-Pelah facing Mamre.... There they buried Abraham and Sarah, his wife; there they buried Isaac and Rebecca, his wife; and there I buried Leah. It is the cave which my grandfather, Abraham, purchased from the sons of Heth.' Then, when Jacob had finished his prophecies to his sons, he lay back in the bed, breathed his last, and died. Joseph threw himself upon his father's body and wept...."

This is the way the average family pictured death at the turn of the century. The dying person was expected to die with dignity, at home, with his family around him. This is the tradition today's older generation grew up with.

In *The View from a Hearse*, Joe Bayly recalls the death of his grandmother. She was at home, and he remembers being allowed to enter her room to pay his last respects and let her say good-bye to him. A few hours later she died, surrounded by her children and grandchildren. In contrast, when his children's grandfather suffered his last heart attack, they saw him carried to an ambulance, rushed to the hospital, and placed in an intensive care unit. He died that night, in strange surroundings, without his family present.

I suspect that this is one of the reasons for the dilemma we face in caring for our dying geriatric patients. They saw death take place with dignity at home. That is the tradition they are familiar with. But their offspring haven't had this experience. Statistics show that at the turn of the century 80 percent of the people died at home, whereas today, 80 percent die in institutions.

Dying in institutions has resulted in two major losses: 1) the individual himself loses his personal dignity as he dies alone in an unfamiliar place, and 2) our entire culture—particularly our young people—have lost sight of death as a personal event. It used to be a natural event; it was part of the family "life," and young people were familiar with it from an early age.

Consequently we have this sad dilemma: the patient wishes for the old days, when death took place at home with the family nearby; but the relatives, having had little experience with death in the family, avoid such contact and have little understanding for the dying person.

Most of us would like to die like Moses. He died when he was 120 years old, full of vigor, eyes undimmed, and still like a young man. He had his successor picked out and trained. He didn't have to worry about who would carry on for him. He didn't have to worry about what would happen to the children of Israel. He met with God and was buried by God in an unknown spot.

After Moses died, a division occurred in the functions of the leader. Moses had been both military leader and priest. But after him, Joshua became the military leader and Eleazar became the priest. The priestly role included being a public health officer and physician. When there was a question about a contagious disease on the skin or in the house, people went to the priest for medical advice. Then eventually, the medical functions separated from the priestly functions.

Today, however, it seems they are being joined again. The physician, whether he likes it or not, has inherited a priestly role in our society which includes "caring for" dying people. Perhaps society has shifted this responsibility to the medical profession because it has redefined man in biological terms only, and seeks biological immortality.

But I submit that most doctors do not believe in a mere biological form of life. Today, for the first time in history, we are able to maintain the biological existence of man by machine. But I have yet to meet a doctor who wants to see a patient stay in that state for any period of time. They would rather see the machine turned off if there is no evidence of mental function—i.e., what some may call the mind and what others may call the soul. In this tacit way, if in no other, they admit that man is more than his physical body.

The spiritual dimension of death appears also in man's universal fear of it. Hebrews 2:14–15 states that Jesus died so that He might "free those who all their lives were held in slavery by their *fear of death.*" We fear the unknown and, those of us who are familiar with the problems of old age, fear the loss of our mental and physical powers which comes as a prelude to death.

Shakespeare described that prelude well in *As You Like It*. He pictures man's life as consisting of seven ages.

> The sixth age shifts
> Into the lean and slippered Pantaloon\*
> With spectacles on nose and pouch on side,
> His youthful hose, well saved, a world too wide
> For his shrunk shank, and his big manly voice,
> Turning again toward childish treble, pipes
> And whistles in his sound. Last scene of all,

---

\* The foolish old man of Italian comedy.

That ends this strange eventful history,
Is second childishness and mere oblivion,
Sans teeth, sans eyes, sans taste, sans everything.

(Act II, Scene 7)

Today the medical profession calls this state the organic mental syndrome. The lay person calls it senility. But whatever we call it, it is a fact that most people will exhibit some of these characteristics if they get into the upper age bracket. Usually they come on gradually: loss of memory for recent events, loss of memory for past events, loss of orientation to surroundings, and finally loss of orientation to the person. And then there is the equally disconcerting fact that older people may leave their bodies exposed from time to time. They may lose control of the primitive functions of defecation and urination. They may need some aid in eating.

It can be very threatening to medical personnel and relatives to see this deterioration occurring. In fact I have observed them time and again actually denying that such a process was taking place. They fear that they will go through a similar deterioration when "their time comes," and they can't bear to admit it.

This is quite understandable. Few of us learn to share so intensely with another human being that we can bare our total personality and body to that person, let alone to strangers. And we fear having our mental defenses down so low that someone else can actually see some of the inner workings of our mind, including thoughts that we might have repressed or suppressed in younger years.

But we must face up to this possibility. The

chances are we will live to old age, we will go through at least some of the stages of senility and, unless the present trend reverses itself, we will probably die in an institution. Does this bleak prospect give us any clue as to how we might minister to those who are in that situation now?

My wife recently met a young woman who had taken care of her husband as he died over a period of months. After he died she became a volunteer, sharing her time in hospitals with others who were in the dying process. The insight she gained as she took care of her husband has given her a real feeling for dying patients.

It is this kind of caring, this kind of concern that dying patients need. I would like to see training courses set up for nurses, doctors, aides, and the volunteers who help to take care of these people. And I would like to see Christians be in the vanguard of such a work. They, of all people, have the resources of true knowledge and understanding which are needed to help those in the valley of the shadow of death. On occasion it will mean sharing the full truth of their knowledge of Christ. Often it will entail just giving a cup of cold water in His name. But however it is expressed, true compassion will lend dignity, personality, and comfort even to a hospital room.

Chapter 10

## IS SUICIDE AN ANSWER?

### By Ray C. Stedman

WHY DO people commit suicide? Less than half of those taking their own life leave notes behind to explain why. Those who do explain why usually imply that they have taken the step because of a desire in some way to "end it all." Life, for them, has become too empty, or too hard, or too fearful to continue. And so they jump off a bridge, turn on the gas, swallow poison, leap in front of a car or train, pull a trigger, hang themselves, or in some other way take their own life rather than face the problems of living any longer.

Do they find the release they are looking for? Does suicide really solve anything? This matter is not an easy one to discuss. But the suicide rate is rising as the tensions of modern life increase, and the prevalence of the problem drives us to the Word of God for counsel and wisdom.

One thing is immediately sure—suicide doesn't "end it all." When we say, "So and so took his own life," we can be very sure that that is the one thing he cannot do. In Matthew 10:28 the Lord Jesus told His disciples, "Fear not them which kill the

## Is Suicide an Answer?

body, but are not able to kill the soul." Certainly this covers all forms of murder, including the murder of one's own self. It is only the body which dies; the soul, or life, goes on.

If, as in the case of most of us, our troubles really lie in the self-life, then it is obvious that a suicide takes with him all the problems and troubles he is so desperately trying to escape. Certain circumstances may be relieved, but the essential problem survives the death of the body because it is linked inescapably to the soul.

This brings up the question: Where does the soul of a suicide go? In answering this from the Scriptures, we must speak separately of the saved and the unsaved.

We have, in the Bible, one terrible record of the suicide of an unbeliever—Judas Iscariot. And it is Christ Himself who tells us what happened to Judas after his suicide. At the Last Supper He said, with great sorrow, "Woe to that man by whom the Son of man is betrayed! good it were for that man if he had never been born." In other words, to have never come into existence at all would have been preferable to what Judas entered into at death.

Hebrews 9:27 tells us that for every man, there will be a judgment after death. "It is appointed unto men once to die, but after this the judgment." I read of one young man who was saved from suicide by this very verse. The thought of a judgment lying beyond death stayed his hand and helped him to take up the battle of life anew. For the unbeliever, that judgment can only result in damnation. And if he has died by his own hand, then the sin for which he is being judged will be just so much the greater.

But what about the suicide of the believer? This

is obviously a much more complex problem. Some Christians feel that it is impossible for a true believer to commit suicide. By taking his own life, he seals his eternal doom; he proves his unbelief.

The great theologian, Dr. William G. T. Shedd, writes: "Suicide, if the act of sanity, is *ipso facto* proof of insubmission and rebellion towards God, and impenitence in sin."

The key words in this statement are "if the act of sanity." In the case of Christian suicides there is often good evidence of insanity or temporary derangement from grief, or fear, or some circumstance in which the person could not rightly be held accountable. Certainly in such cases salvation would never be in doubt for it is guaranteed by the blood of Jesus Christ, and the blood of suicide cannot alter it.

"But," someone says, "suppose a Christian deliberately plans his suicide in order to escape what he thinks is an intolerable condition? Is he not better off in heaven than on earth?" The answer to this is the apostle's words in 1 Cor. 3:15, "... he shall suffer loss, but he himself shall be saved, yet so as by fire."

Do not pass lightly over those words, "suffer loss." They mean a great deal indeed. Such a suicide is a deliberate act of rebellion against the Creator. By it, the one in question is saying to God, "I refuse to accept Your choice for my life. I will not tolerate the conditions You have put me in!" Such rebellion must be quelled before any degree of fellowship with God is possible. The scourging of the Father is in order for such a one. Specifically what God does to correct this is not revealed. Who knows what agonies of shame and heartache are hidden in those words, "Suffer loss"?

Certainly it may be asked, "Can a life which ends in defeat here possibly begin in victory over there?" The apostle Peter speaks of "giving diligence to make your calling and election sure . . . for so an entrance shall be ministered unto you *abundantly* into the everlasting kingdom of our Lord and Savior, Jesus Christ." The entrance into the everlasting kingdom is purchased for us by Christ; the degree of abundance is dependent on us. What kind of an entrance can a suicide have?

Besides the rebellion and willfulness which must be dealt with at the judgment seat of Christ, and besides the tears and sorrow, the uprooted lives, and the unending shame left as a legacy to those behind, each would-be suicide should face the loss he accrues in his failure to fight the battle of life through to the end appointed of God. Paul could write, "This light affliction, which is but for a moment, worketh for us a far more exceeding and eternal weight of glory." Whatever that weight of glory signifies (and surely it must be supremely worthwhile), it seems to be related directly to the degree of affliction we suffer in this world. In another place the apostle says, "For I reckon that the sufferings of this present time are not worthy to be compared with the glory that shall be revealed in us." Ah, but what if we refuse the sufferings? Is there not a corresponding loss in glory?

Doubtless the worst thing of all, for the Christian suicide, will be the eternal knowledge, the haunting certainty throughout eternity, that it wasn't necessary! No Christian ever needs to commit suicide. God knows indeed that the trials are sometimes sore and hard to bear—but what of His promises?

Everyone tempted to suicide should read often

Isaiah 43:2, "When thou passest through the waters, I will be with thee; and through the rivers, they shall not overflow thee; when thou walkest through the fire, thou shalt not be burned, neither shall the flame kindle upon thee." Other great passages for times of stress are Psalm 23, Psalm 62, Hebrews 12:1-3, and 4:14-16.

Perhaps no greater temptation to suicide can come than to face the prospect of years of pain and suffering, shut up within the four walls of a sickroom. Yet even in such extreme testing, the grace of God can triumph.

"No temptation has seized you," wrote the Apostle Paul, "except what is common to man. And God is faithful; he will not let you be tempted beyond what you can bear. But when you are tempted, he will also provide a way out so that you can stand up under it" (I Cor. 10:13).

CHAPTER 11

# *HOW A CHRISTIAN FIGHTS SUICIDE*

Anonymous

FOR YEARS I have read articles on the Christian and suicide, but I have yet to come across one that touches the heart of the matter. Most dwell on the cowardice of suicide. Some claim that the act of suicide proves that the person could not really have been born from above; at the very best, he was insane.

Yet much more can be said on this subject. The temptation to suicide comes to many a troubled pilgrim. Perhaps if Christians had a deeper understanding of the matter, there would be fewer deaths of this nature among Christians. But it is a subject we naturally avoid. It is shrouded in an aura of shame, and we contemplate it only in the privacy of our own world of thought. And so the help which could come from open discussion is lost.

I know whereof I speak. I have been chronically ill from childhood. Increasingly, I suffer seizures of desperate pain which doctors cannot alleviate, let alone prevent or cure. I am never free from weariness. It is hard even to imagine a feeling of physical well-being. On top of this, I have never known normal family love. Consequently, the spectre of suicide has peered over my shoulder many times. Although I have been an earnest Christian since youth, I never know when I shall be called upon to do mortal combat with this grim Adversary.

I was past forty before I once mentioned this problem to anybody, and then it was to my Christian physician. It seems that even Christian ministers are horrified to think that a fellow-believer could be tempted in such a way. I have fought my most desolate battles alone, and I give all the glory to God for keeping me from this grievous sin. But oh, if the troubled spirit could but pour out its anguish to another believing soul, could but grasp the hand of fellowship and faith rather than shrink from censorious recoil, how much easier could be the road to victory!

The Christian who would help one who is tempted with thoughts of suicide must first of all be sympathetic. There can be not even a trace of shock or surprise. If you have never sat where the sufferer sits, you may never be able really to understand his problem. But you must earnestly seek the Spirit's enlightening aid, and must not in any way condemn if you would be used of God to bring release to his troubled soul.

You must recognize the fact that this temptation is not in itself sin. The soul in such trouble needs urgently to talk his problem out with another believer. When faced in the light, and in fellowship, the powers of darkness and loneliness lose much of their strength. This is one of God's appointed ways of delivering His tempted children; it is unspeakable pity that so few Christians are themselves spiritually equipped to deal with the soul haunted by suicide.

## How a Christian Fights Suicide

Many practical things can help. Don't spend too much time talking over the pros and cons of the matter; the life situations that give rise to such temptations are usually very real, and can seldom be resolved by mere talk. But you can make the sufferer aware of your sympathetic interest; your understanding, insofar as you have it; above all, your friendship, your willingness to stand by. You can seek to give him something definite to do—some work geared to his abilities, which may be sharply limited, since physical frailties so often play a major part in such trouble. But give him a missionary to write to, a needy home to visit, a book to read. Call him often; invite him to lunch; go for a walk with him. Keep him conscious of your compassion, your love, your readiness to be "one called alongside to help." And supremely, seek to build up within him an awareness of God, and to strengthen his general spiritual life.

How? Let me share some of the spiritual truths which the Holy Spirit has taught me, by means of which He has strengthened me to resist this sometimes almost overwhelming temptation.

It is not the cowardice of suicide that comes foremost in my thinking: one may fight with unfaltering courage for many years, and yet go down in one desperate moment. Surely the Judge of all the earth, who shall do right, will not let that one moment of cowardice—if that is what it is—overwrite the long decades of pain or sorrow nobly born, and name that soul only coward.

To me, it is not the preciousness of the gift of life that makes suicide a sin, for the cold fact is, as thousands of doctors can attest, that for some people physical life may be, and is, an almost intolerable burden, infinitely harder to bear than to lay down.

Neither is it the fact that suicide is sin which gives me pause in the face of black temptation, telling as that is to one who truly loves his Lord. I am not convinced that this is the most serious sin of which the Christian may be guilty. Hatred, bitterness, malice, unforgiveness—these, and other such evils with their tragic inter-mingling and ever-widening circles of woes, frequently visited upon innocent children, may one day be judged more harshly than one desolate, desperate sin of self-destruction.

No, there are reasons far deeper and stronger than these for striving unto blood against the dark Enemy, and Christians who would learn to deliver tempted souls must think beyond these superficialities. Indeed, we would all do well to give earnest thought to these matters, for one never knows when the grim spectre of suicide may knock at his own door.

I think what has helped me most is a deep and growing understanding of the doctrine of the Sovereignty of God. A stern remedy to offer one whose heart and mind are obviously in poor condition to receive it, you say. Yet severe illnesses require stern remedies. Have you experienced the power of this doctrine in your own life? Perhaps if more Christians had, they would be better able to apply it as a remedy for others.

To me the Sovereignty of God has become an all-embracing Haven of Refuge. What God is: that great pulsing, giving Heart of love and wisdom, whose infinite tenderness and measureless self-sacrifice are so palpably ours in Bethlehem and Calvary—that awareness, growing in scope and preciousness with the years, has, for me, quite overshadowed the questions that His inscrutable providences in my own life call forth. *"This God"*—and everything depends on what lies behind that little word, "this"—*"this* God," "infinite, eternal and unchangeable in His being, wisdom, power, holiness, justice, goodness and truth"—*"this* God is *my* God for ever and ever." This is the unshaken and, pray God, unshakeable conviction of my soul; my shelter in the time of storm.

When everything he owned was swept away in one sudden stroke of desolation by the God he loved and unfailingly served, we read of Job that "he fell down and worshipped." And so it must ever be. The soul that knows God for what He truly is cannot but acknowledge His Sovereignty, can only bow and worship, no matter what He may send. This, in essence, is the strongest, perhaps the only real reason why a Christian cannot commit suicide; and he who would help the tempted soul must seek to bring him to such a realization, in dependence on the Holy Spirit.

But there are other reasons. God has invested His honor in His saints. The Eternal God, Creator and Sustainer of the Universe, whom angels delight to worship, before whom seraphim and cherubim continually do cry, "Holy, holy, holy, Lord God Almighty," has seen fit to entrust His honor, the glory of His Name, the immutability of His Word, to the frail, erring, but believing sons of earth. The soul tempted to suicide, in a peculiar sense, holds that inestimable wonder in his trembling hands. This is why the Adversary so frequently tempts in this way.

To one who truly knows God, His honor is unspeakably precious. Oftentimes the reminder of that sacred trust is enough to turn the force of the Tempter's blow. For His Name's sake, His Word's sake, His glory's sake, God so often in Old Testament story turned away His wrath from His sinning children. For His Name's sake, His Word's sake, His holy honor's sake, His child who truly loves Him will suffer, will bear, will endure, will refuse to do the final evil that would irrevocably proclaim to earth and heaven and hell His insufficiency.

When Abraham, though ninety years of age, had yet not received the thrice-promised son, God revealed Himself as El-Shaddai, the All-Sufficient, the Satisfier, the Nourisher, the Strength-Giver, the God Who is Enough. So to the soul grown old in suffering, not having received the promise of deliverance and knowing well that it can never be his this side of Eternity, God is still El-Shaddai, the God Who is Enough. In that strength we must live; and the honor of that promise, God's own honor, than which He has no higher gift to bestow, invested in our weak and aching bodies and faltering, weary hearts, we must defend against Satan to the end. Not to everyone is such high and terrible mission given. If it is ours, we must know that even for this, there is a God Who is Enough; and to that end we must seek His grace.

When Saul, smitten to his knees, tremblingly asked, "What wilt Thou have me to *do*?" God sent him a strange answer. "I will show ... what things he must *suffer* for My sake." It is human to want to do for God; it is godlike to learn to suffer for His sake. Even the Savior, "though He were a Son, yet learned He obedience by the things which He suffered." So often it is to those seemingly best qualified by nature to do for God—the most sensitive, perceptive spirits, the keenest minds, the most artistic, creative souls—that this strange command comes instead to suffer; and life becomes one unending battle of frustration. To many such souls comes Satan with the suggestion of Giant Despair: "Why should you choose life, since it is attended with so much bitterness?" Instead of the sacrifice of service, we are asked to give the sacrifice of praise even while being denied all that is natural and right and good. Yet such sacrifice, if offered up with a true heart willingly (and only those who must do it day in, day out, can know how hard this is!), finds its holy way to the very throne of God Himself. And who can tell but what it may bring more joy to the heart of the Father than all the service offered by others in strength and gladness? But such devotion must not be cut short before its time if it is to reach its full fruition.

The last point is, to me, most pertinent of all. Our eternal destiny and reward is now being shaped. Our capacity for God, now being formed by the hammer and chisel of these God-given, seemingly cruel circumstances, *and by our attitude to them*, is that in which we shall one day glorify God and enjoy Him forever. Should we terminate our time of enlarging that capacity, who can measure our eternal loss? For while in Heaven all shall be filled with the fulness of God, shall not the souls with the greater capacity have the greater fulness?

Our future service for God depends on our present faithfulness, whether in service or suffering. If we cut short our time of training, the celestial service for which He would have schooled us must pass to another. To him that is faithful in little— and in the vast, undimmed light of Eternity we shall know, as He knows, that our present trials are indeed little compared to the glory that shall be revealed—to him shall much be entrusted. God keep us faithful to the end!

And finally, we must meet Him both as Savior and Judge. How shall we enter His presence unbidden, how look upon His face uncalled for, with that last, dread, and necessarily unconfessed sin upon our hearts? Having striven and endured so long for His "Well done, My good and faithful servant, enter thou into the joy of thy Lord," shall we not endure to the end? For "he that shall endure to the end shall be saved"—saved to the glory of His "Welcome Home," to the blessedness of His presence; filled to all fulness with His very Self; filled to the God-designed and God-perfected capacity for Him for which He has chosen us before the foundation of the world.

Chapter 12

# *WHAT SHALL I TELL MY CHILD?*

By Ellis Guthrie

Anybody who loves his child wants to shield him from the unpleasant facts of life: war, divorce, crime, death. But of course we can't shield him forever, and if we aren't around to explain these things to him, somebody else will.

How do you tell a child about death? Partly, of course, it depends on the child's age. The secret is to share only as much as he is ready to receive. Frances L. Ilg and Louise Bates Ames, in one of their syndicated columns, wrote of the child, "He can accept and adapt to what little we know and don't know of life after death if we are considerate of his early immaturity and do not present too much uncertainty, or brutal fact, too soon."

Let's look at the problems. What about grief? Should children be allowed to see their parents weep, or should tears be suppressed when they are around?

Grief in the face of death can be a healthy thing. It is human. If the child sees his parents weeping, he understands better what death is. He understands that his parents can be hurt or disappointed, and he identifies with them. The hard part is that in their grief, they are showing him how he should handle his as he grows up. If grief takes the form of uncontrolled weeping, fear, or hysteria, the child's whole attitude toward death may be warped. No matter how much they tell him about the Christian's hope of eternal life, their undisciplined grieving tells him it really isn't true.

Another problem is the question of whether or not to allow the child to see the corpse. Some people argue that if a child sees a corpse, it will cause unhealthy fears to develop which will follow him through life. But this is largely dependent upon the attitudes of adults. He picks up their attitudes; they teach him how to feel by the way they react. Actually, childhood is the best time to gain an understanding and a wholesome view of death. If a parent deliberately postpones it, he may be putting it off to a time when it may well be more of a shock than it would have been earlier.

I believe that a child under five has but little impression when seeing a corpse. Death is not understandable to him except in terms of life, for example, of heaven. Even children up to ten weep at a funeral only because adults weep. They are still learning about death.

Helen and Lewis Sherrill in an article, "Interpreting Death to Children," write, "Between about five and nine it was found that a child tends to personify death, not yet accepting it as a final process. Not until around the age of nine did a child first begin to recognize death as inevitable for all persons, and as something that can come to *him*."

Let this set the tone for the kind of teaching we give to our children.

A third consideration is the way we explain

## What Shall I Tell My Child? 81

death to our children. As Christians we should keep our explanation grounded in the truth of Scripture. Parents need to help children understand God's mastery over death without placing the responsibility for it on Him.

Several approaches can be made. If it is an elderly person who has died, the child can better understand that it has been a blessing for that one to die. God has taken him from a life of pain and the infirmities of old age to a life of unending joy in heaven.

If the death has been caused by an accident, the parents can explain it in terms of the disarray of our world, caused by sin. God is busy bringing order out of the chaos that man has made through his mistakes and misdeeds. Sometimes man brings death upon himself or on another by his carelessness or sin. Man must obey God's laws if life is to be long and good.

As children grow older, they will begin to wonder how a person lives when his body dies. An explanation which I have used with good results is this. "When we lived in a former pastorate," I explained to our children, "the house was old and unsatisfactory. When we moved out, it was dead—no life in it. But we were still alive. Then we moved into our present home. It is much bigger and nicer. So it is in death. We get a new home. We go to heaven to live with Jesus. We leave our old home—our body—for awhile, but then some day Jesus will make it gloriously new. And from that new body we will never again have to move."

Finally, however, parents must be free to admit that they do not have all the answers. Actually, if we occasionally admit our ignorance, it seems to increase our children's confidence in us, rather than diminish it.

If we teach our children by example as well as by word, they will accept by faith God's eternal goodness, even in the face of events that seem to have no rhyme nor reason. We can help them face death calmly, and give them a heritage for which they shall be forever grateful.

CHAPTER 13

# WHAT I TELL THE PARENTS OF A DYING CHILD

By C. Everett Koop

WHEN AN elderly person dies, grief is sometimes assuaged by the knowledge that the person has had a long life or one rich in achievement. Death may even be welcomed by both the elderly patient and the family as surcease from pain or disability. But none of these rationalizations applies when the dying patient is a child. Then death seems totally unacceptable, to families and doctors alike.

Quite early in my career as a pediatric surgeon, I decided that the problem of the incurable child was one that we doctors had to face directly and honestly; and that we had to do something to help the parents as well as the child.

Our responsibility does not end with doing our professional best; we have to provide support and reassurance as well. We have to be a humane link between the family and the unknown.

The least bearable loss is that of a child who dies from an incurable disease. There is a shock when a child is killed in an accident. There is grief when a baby is born with a congenital defect which even the most skillful surgery cannot repair. But such grief is mitigated by the fact that the baby may not live more than a few days. However, it is sheer agony not only to the family but to the entire community, and to the staff of the hospital, when a child is lost with a malignant tumor or with leukemia.

I remember vividly the first time I had to face this problem, more than twenty years ago. It was a day when I was torn between joy and sorrow: the day my first son was born and the day I had to tell a family that they were going to lose theirs—a five-year-old who had just undergone an operation for a malignant tumor.

We met in their child's private room, and I had to tell them that, to the best of my ability to understand the situation, I did not see how we would be able to save their child's life. I also told them that we would do everything we could to ease their lives during the coming months, and to guard their child against pain and suffering.

Some instinct told me to keep on talking, and I have since learned that this is the right thing to do. For as I did so, they were able to absorb the impact of that first awful blow. I told them everything I knew about the diagnosis and the prognosis. Then I excused myself and left them alone to pull themselves together. When I came back, their eyes were red but they had made their first adjustment to their loss.

Of course, telling the truth includes a tiny ray of hope even in the most desperate cases. In one such case, a boy was brought to us with a suspected abdominal tumor. When we operated, we found a large unencapsulated neuroblastoma, a malignancy common in young children. I took out what I

## What I Tell the Parents of a Dying Child

could, but finished the operation with a hopeless feeling of failure, knowing that some cancer cells remained in the child's body. Then I spoke to the parents, telling them that the situation appeared to be out of control. "If he were my own child," I said, "I wouldn't subject him to X-ray or drug treatments. I would take him home and make his death as comfortable as possible."

That was nineteen years ago. Today that patient is a student at a midwestern university. His last X-ray examination showed absolutely no evidence of disease.

There are just enough of such unexplained spontaneous remissions in children's cancer to justify leaving the door of hope open a crack. At the same time, we have to be careful not to arouse false expectations in parents because their eventual despair will then be even greater. The family may even become disillusioned with medicine and develop attitudes toward it which will deprive them or their other children of proper treatment later on.

Because most people feel that doctors don't tell them everything, I try to be as candid as possible. The first thing I say to the parents of a sick child before an operation is: "You and I have to work together to help your child, and we can't do that if you don't trust me. So I'm not going to pull any punches even though these things may be hard for you to take. But rest assured that tomorrow in the operating room I'm going to treat your child exactly as I would want one of mine treated. And after it's all over, I'll tell you what I've found and what I think."

After the operation, which may take hours, the parents' nerves are raw and they must be treated gently. I have learned that the worst moment for the parents is when they finally understand that the child's condition is grave. It is certainly worse than the death itself, for by that time they will have become reconciled to its inevitability.

I try to answer questions before they are asked. Long experience tells me that inevitably the parents will want to know: "How long?" "Will he be well again for a time?" "Can he go back to school?" "Will he suffer much?" and "Is there any hope?"

And I also know that there are certain pitfalls that the family must be warned against: the people who will tell them about a man with a uranium mine where patients can sit and be cured of cancer, or the "doctor" with a revolving chair and green lights who has a "sure" cure.

"If there were any such effective treatment, believe me, I'd know about it," I assure them. "And if there were some other hospital that could help your child more than we can, I'd send you there."

I encourage questions about these things because too many families have fallen into the hands of cancer "remedy" peddlers who take their house and car and leave them nothing but disappointment, and who will put their child through unnecessary pain without helping him in any way. We've seen this happen in spite of our best efforts. We have known people who mortgaged their homes to provide useless nostrums for their children. And, of course, the children died anyway.

Because we have a number of anticancer drugs today that we did not have twenty years ago, and because we know much more about the management of childhood cancer than we did, I often can talk honestly to parents in hopeful terms. But the hope may not be permanent. Drugs which may save

## What I Tell the Parents of a Dying Child 87

some lives may merely prolong life in a child who might have died weeks or months sooner.

As I am writing this, I am dreading the visit of a mother whose child was first brought to us two years ago, with a tumor which had spread to bone. We could see it on X ray, and even feel it. In our experience, this type of tumor in this stage is almost always fatal.

Years ago, the boy would have been gone within a few weeks. But under X-ray and drug treatment, his primary tumor shrank from the size of a melon to the size of an orange. We removed it and, almost miraculously, the boy was restored to apparently good health.

With everything going smoothly, one hated to raise the gruesome possibility that this remission might not last. Still, the family had to be prepared for what might happen, so I have been careful to tell them that I've been amazed by the boy's progress, and to make them understand that this is not the same thing as saying I'm perfectly happy with his condition.

Now the drugs are no longer effective. The mother knows it. I know it. But we haven't said it to each other, and we're going to have to say it. After our discussion, I'll suggest that they see their pastor.

We at the hospital try to provide every other type of help—psychological, spiritual and material —that the family needs. For if they can lean on us with confidence, they can support the child better than we can.

Particularly as the end draws near is this so. The family's horizon is closer; I suggest a day-by-day kind of expectation. If the family wants reassurance, I give them reassurance. If they want prayer,

I pray. If they have a false guilt, I try to explain it away. If they are willing, I encourage relationship with their pastor, priest or rabbi, and then I work with him too.

But almost inevitably there comes the moment when they ask, "Why did this have to happen to *my* child?" There is no logical answer. I tell them what I believe: "If I were not completely convinced of the sovereignty of God, I couldn't take care of your child." This thought gives most parents great comfort, just as it has sustained me through my years of practice.

If a family believes in God at all, they believe in a God who is omnipotent and omniscient. Being reminded that God is sovereign, and that the child's fate—even if that is death—is in the hands of God, they are relieved of the burden of personal responsibility and guilt.

Most families then say, "All we can do is hope and pray." My answer is: "We are certainly going to hope as long as we can. But about praying: to whom are you going to pray, and what for?"

"I'm going to pray to God, of course, and I'm going to pray for my child's life." To this I say, "Perhaps you should pray for your child's life *if it is God's will.* But if it is not, then you should pray for the spiritual maturity and stamina to take the difficult times ahead, and to give your child the support that he needs." I believe this helps people realize that there is more to prayer than asking for a gift from Heaven.

After learning of their child's fate, some families decide to have Christmas in July for Johnny, because Johnny isn't going to be here for Christmas. I don't encourage this for two reasons. First, Johnny may well be here for Christmas. And, sec-

## What I Tell the Parents of a Dying Child

ond, any child old enough to reason wants to know why Christmas is coming in July this year, rather than December. Children are quite keen enough not to be fooled in this way.

Sometimes the child himself will ask me: "Doctor, am I going to die?" To a few children who have shown stability and honesty—and have shown that they expect them from me—I have said, "Yes, but we don't know when." This may seem cold-blooded, but I believe it is the right of a child old enough to ask this question to know his fate—if he can assimilate that knowledge. I have never known a child to break down when faced with the fact of his impending death. Children are much stronger than adults in this regard; they can accept about themselves what their elders cannot accept for them.

If we have done everything for a child that science and medicine can do, and the illness cannot be controlled, we ask the parents where they prefer to have the child. Many want him at home; but in families with younger children, the death of a sister or brother may be too much for the others to bear.

So the parents may decide to put the sick child in the hospital, where help is always near. If they do this with one of my patients, I will be in the hospital when he dies. This often means spending nights there, but this is of little importance when balanced against the comfort it gives to parents to know that their child hasn't been abandoned.

I normally write a letter to the parents of a child who has died. In it I remind them of the sovereignty of God, His wisdom and His concern for all of us.

Recently a Roman Catholic priest wrote me that

he had read a copy of my letter to two parents in his congregation whose children were dying.

He said he appreciated this clear statement of faith from a surgeon, and he asked if the local newspaper could republish it. To my surprise, it appeared on page one.

Recently while talking to parents of a child who was going to live but be temporarily inconvenienced with a colostomy, I heard the voice of a mother coming from my secretary's office.

That woman had lost her child, but had found Christ through her son's illness and had strengthened her faith through his death. I asked her to speak to the parents in my office. She said, "If my son had lived his life only so I could have met Dr. Koop, who led me and our family to Jesus Christ, then his life would not have been in vain. But he had eight wonderful years of love from us and we had eight wonderful years of being with him."

Chapter 14

# *WHAT DO I SAY TO SOMEONE WHO'S DYING?*

By Joseph T. Bayly

How would you react if a friend of yours became terminally ill?

Listen in as a husband and wife respond to the news that one of their friends is dying of cancer.

**Wednesday, May 13, 6 p.m.**

"I heard it today. George is going to die. The hospital tests were positive. He has cancer."

"Poor George. And poor Ethel. How soon?"

"Oh, the doctors don't tell you anymore."

"Did you talk to Ethel?"

"Yes, she called me from the hospital."

"How's she taking it?"

"She's broken up. She pleaded with the doctor not to tell George, but the doctor wouldn't hear of it. Said George is a strong person, that he has spiritual roots—or something like that—and not telling him when Ethel knew would only make them play-act during the time that remains."

"Would you want the doctor to tell me if I had cancer?"

"I think so. We've shared everything else in life, why go at that alone?"

"Who'd be alone if I didn't know?"

"Both of us—and at a time when we'd need each other the most. And besides, the doctor said George would know he was going to die, even if he didn't tell him."

"How?"

"That's what Ethel asked the doctor. He said by all the special ways people treat you, by the questions the doctors ask—or don't ask, by the nurses' attitudes, things like that."

"So he told George."

"No, actually he asked Ethel to tell him, or to go with Pastor Ewing while he told him. So she did—after we talked on the phone this afternoon."

"How did George take it?"

"Like I said, they told him after we talked on the phone. So I don't know. But you know George—he'll bounce back."

"I hope so. Maybe I should go in to the hospital to see him—not that I particularly want to."

"Maybe you should. But certainly not tonight. You'd better wait a day or two."

"Poor George. And Ethel."

Friday, May 15, 8:30 P.M.

"What's for supper? I'm starving!"

"I'll have it on in a few minutes. It's in the oven. I didn't know when to expect you. How's George?"

"I was really surprised. He didn't want to talk about his sickness, just about getting back to his job and his garden. It was almost as if he didn't know he had cancer and was going to die."

"I hope you didn't—"

"No, I didn't. I just fitted in with his mood. We

## What Do I Say to Someone Who's Dying?

also talked about fishing, and about what needs to be done at their summer place. We didn't talk about anything serious, really.

"Ethel is worried about his reaction. She stopped in this afternoon, after she'd been to the hospital. She says George seems blissfully unaware that anything's wrong. She asked their doctor about it and he said not to get uptight—George was sort of denying what he'd been told, what he really knows deep down inside. But that isn't all bad, the doctor says—it lets George sort of mobilize his resources for the battle ahead."

"I still guess I'd feel better if he'd face up to the future and you could discuss it with him."

"You'd feel better, but maybe he'd feel worse."

### Sunday, May 24, 4 P.M.

"How do you feel about George and Ethel?"

"Upset. I almost wish we hadn't gone to the hospital to see him. How do you feel?"

"The same way. I never expected George to say the things he said this afternoon."

"Do you mean his complaining about the doctors and nurses?"

"That too, but mainly what he said about God. He sounded almost bitter. Or at least angry at God for the fact that he has cancer."

"I was disturbed at that, too. After all, George is a Christian and ought to be on top of this instead of asking 'Why?' the way he did. 'Why me, when I'm only fifty-two years old?'"

"Yes, and when he said, 'Why does Ethel have to be left a widow?' And you only upset him when you asked if he didn't think God knew what He was doing."

"Ethel too. She pitched right in to defend

George, and, in fact, said that was exactly the way she felt, too."

"I guess what really ticked me off was him saying he'd always been taught that God is love, but now he can only see God as vengeful—if God is in this thing at all."

"He didn't say 'vengeful'—he said 'the farthest thing from love.'"

"Whatever he said. And when he said why did God let him be married at all, if he was going to have to leave a widow behind to face the future."

"I was glad to hear that he'll be going home the first of next week. Maybe he's just been in the hospital too long. It'll be a relief to be back in his own home, and it'll be a relief to Ethel to have him there. These trips to the hospital every day for almost two weeks must have worn her out."

### Thursday, May 28, 6:30 P.M.

"I went over to see George and Ethel this afternoon. He came home from the hospital Tuesday."

"How are they?"

"I'm not really sure. The pastor came just after I did, and so I didn't stay very long."

"Are they still bitter?"

"They were sort of quiet, although George at one point did ask the pastor why God would let such an awful thing happen to him."

"What did the pastor say?"

"Not much. He didn't seem surprised, or shocked, but just said that there are some things in life that are mysteries that we may never fully understand. But we have to remember that God loves us."

"Seems to me that he should have gotten after George for questioning God."

## What Do I Say to Someone Who's Dying? 95

**Tuesday, August 21, 10 P.M.**

"Ethel came over this afternoon. I think she wanted to talk to someone."

"What did she say?"

"George wants to go to some healing meetings that are being held out at the fairgrounds. She says he promised God he'd do anything God wanted him to if He'd just let him live another five years."

"Is she going to take him?"

"Yes, I think so. He's pretty weak—doesn't get out much any more. But she thinks he's up to a trip like that, even so."

"We could go along to help."

"I told her that, but there's this couple who live across the street from them, who've been telling them it's not God's will for George to die—that God wants to heal him, if he and Ethel only have faith. They're going to take them out to the meeting."

"Where do they get their information that God doesn't want George to die—that He doesn't plan to take him Home?"

"You don't think I'd ask her that, do you? I just said that if George wanted to go, I'd surely see that he got there, if I were her."

"I guess you're right."

**Saturday, August 25, 10 A.M.**

"That was Ethel on the phone. She says they went to the healing meeting last night. George went forward for prayer, and he's a different man this morning. He ate a good breakfast, and is out in the garden doing some things right now. Ethel is so happy."

"Isn't that great. I hope it keeps up."

"Don't be cynical."

## Friday, August 31, 4:30 p.m.

"Hello, dear. I wanted to catch you before you left the office for home. They took George back to the hospital today. He's pretty sick—they may have to operate. I thought maybe you'd like to stop at the hospital to see him on your way home from work."

"Yes, I guess I would. This must be quite a blow to him."

"It is, according to Ethel. And to her too. After they were so sure that...."

"Keep supper for me, dear."

"I will."

## 9:00 p.m.

"Hello, I'm home."

"I'm upstairs. I'll be right down."

"Don't hurry."

"I'll have supper on the table in a few minutes. How was George?"

"Terribly depressed. About all he said was, 'I'm going to die, I'm going to leave Ethel behind,' and then he began to cry. Ethel seemed sort of numb."

"What did you say?"

"What could I say? It wasn't a time for words. I just sat there with them until visiting hours were over. Then I prayed very briefly for them, that God would give them strength and reassure them of His love."

"I think you did exactly right."

"The doctors have decided against surgery."

## Thursday, September 20, 6 p.m.

"I stopped at the hospital during lunch hour today. It was one of the hardest things I've ever done."

"Was Ethel there?"

"Yes, the past few days she has spent most of her time at the hospital. George has really gone downhill—the end can't be far off now."

"Was George upset?"

"No, actually he seemed quite peaceful. He didn't say anything to me the whole time I was there."

"Was he unconscious?"

"No, he knew what was going on. He just held Ethel's hand and looked up at her face."

"What made it such a difficult time?"

"I guess I felt guilty, coming into the room there in good health, with my job to return to, and with you at home—whereas he'll soon lose everything that he hasn't already lost. And guilty about Ethel, too. That her world is coming apart."

"But he will be going home to Jesus. So it's not really loss for George."

"Even so, he'll be leaving Ethel behind. But like I said, surprisingly, he seemed to have found peace."

"Dear George, I'm glad. It must be easier for Ethel, too. That he can accept death, I mean."

"Yes, she seems at peace the same as he does. And she sincerely seemed to appreciate my visit."

"Did you say anything?"

"I read the first part of John 14 and the twenty-third Psalm from my pocket Testament. Then I prayed for them. Just before I left, George took my hand for a moment."

"There goes the phone, I'll answer it."

## Comment

Dr. Elisabeth Kübler-Ross, a psychiatrist who has done pioneering work in the area of understanding dying people and their families (*On Death and Dying*, Macmillan), describes five "stages of dying": denial, anger, bargaining, depression and acceptance. These are illustrated, in this order, by the experience of George and Ethel—an experience that flows more evenly than most of real life. Ideally, the dying person and his family pass through these stages in tandem; this is observed, with the exception of the first stage, in George and Ethel's reactions.

Do Christians go through these stages? Yes, although—as with those who are not Christians— they may not experience some stages, including final acceptance. (Certain Psalms of David and reactions of Job indicate a similar pattern.)

Now what about our own response to the dying person and his family? Here George and Ethel's friends both measure up yet fall short of being most supportive.

They are sensitive to George and Ethel's needs, and do not hold back from getting involved. (A surprising number of people do avoid involvement, often because they don't know how to respond to grief and loss. This can only increase the loneliness and suffering of those who approach the death incident.)

"Sit with me, hold my hand," a young woman with a terminal illness once wrote. "I'm not looking for answers, I just want to know that you'll be there when I need you."

The doctor and pastor are also sensitive, wise people in this example. The doctor refuses to withhold the diagnosis of malignancy from George, recognizing the disastrous consequences of "play-acting." He is also wise in enlisting the pastor's help in telling George the diagnosis. A doctor and pastor make a great team when they cooperate.

Both of them are a help to Ethel in relieving her concern over George's initial denial of death, and in not making George and Ethel feel guilty when they later become angry at what they feel God has done to them.

George and Ethel's friends fail to understand their situation, however, when they are critical of this reaction of anger and resentment. We Christians are not always "on top of" a deteriorating situation, especially such a serious one as approaching death and consequent separation—even though we know the future will bring reunion.

This incident does not imply that God never heals a terminally ill person, one who is about to die. It does show that Christians are not immune to the bargaining stage, and that Christian bargaining with God sometimes takes the form of attendance at healing meetings, often through the suggestion of well-meaning friends who have a conviction "from God" that it is not His will for the person to die.

George's friend is at his best at the very end, when both George and Ethel have reached the stage of acceptance. He does not try to get George to talk; he senses that George has nothing more to say. He reads two brief, familiar and loved passages, prays a final prayer, shows his loving concern in a final grip of the hand.

Have you experienced such a situation? If you have, you know the tragic beauty—and privilege—of helping your friend pack his bags for the last and greatest trip. And you know the sense of peace afterward as you move to help ease your friend's loved ones in their transition into a new life.

A tough assignment?

"I can do all things through Christ, who strengthens me" (Phil. 4:13).

## Chapter 15

## *HOW NOT TO BE A MISERABLE COMFORTER*

By Marjorie Brumme

Our mission as Christians is to "weep with those who weep" (Rom. 12:15). But it has been my experience that it is infinitely easier for Christians to obey the first half of that verse—"Rejoice with those who rejoice." Only those who have themselves been comforted by God are able to share that comfort. To fake it, or simulate it, is cruel. Too often we have to cry to our friends as Job did to his, "Miserable comforters are you all!"

The death of two of our children in five years' time stunned the members and friends of our church as well as us. In trying to explain it, I am afraid that many times we felt like Job. His friends, with their finite minds, were trying to explain God's ways with him: perhaps he wasn't spiritual enough, or maybe he was being punished for some unconfessed sin. But who knows the mind of God? Who can explain His dealings with the children of men? If our hearts condemn us not, then who can say that our difficulties and sorrows are a punishment for sin?

Then, too, if we have never had to face sorrow or

tragedy in our own life, it is easy to equate self-control with spirituality. Because it makes us uncomfortable to be around one who is sorrowing, we can quickly say of him, if he happens to show his emotion, "He must not have the victory!" or "He must not be very spiritual!"

Shortly after the death of our five-year-old son, an evangelist friend said to me, "I know your husband has the victory. Have you?" I was stunned. I really didn't know how to answer him. Victory? How can victory heal a broken heart? A month later, this same man had a complete nervous breakdown. We didn't see him again for several years, but when we did he said, "It took my breakdown to give me a compassionate heart. When I spoke with you last, I said foolish things."

If calamity does not come to us, it does not mean that we are any higher on the scale of spirituality than someone whom it does strike. It may indicate the opposite. When God purposes to use somebody, He will probably put him through some severe training. As someone else has put it:

"Do you wonder why you are passing through some special sorrow? Wait until ten years are passed, and you will find many afflicted as you are. You will tell them how you have suffered, and have been comforted, then as the tale is unfolded, and the soothing anodyne is applied, which God once wrapped around you, in the eager look, and the gleam of hope that shall chase the shadow of despair across the soul, you will know why you were afflicted, and bless God that stored your life with such a fund of experience and helpfulness."

Death is not the only sorrow. Many are the hearts which have broken over wayward sons and daughters, or unfaithful husbands or wives. I can

## How Not to be a Miserable Comforter

never forget the words of one of our dear deacons, at the graveside of our seventeen-year-old daughter. He said, "There are sorrows worse than death." We understood only too well what he was referring to as we thought of his own daughter, mentally retarded, who had lived for years, a burden to the family. We could understand too the tender loving compassion he had for all those in sorrow.

But what if we have never had to experience deep sorrow? Is there no way we can comfort another? Yes, there is, as long as we don't try to sound wiser than we are. Here are a few suggestions:

First, ask God to give you a tender heart.

Second, a knowledge of God's Word is a must, for in that is the only true comfort. I will never forget how the Twenty-third Psalm came alive to me after the death of our first child. I had known it by heart for many years, but it did not become real until then.

Third, be willing to give of yourself and your time if necessary. A missionary friend told me of how she had spent two days with a friend whose husband had just passed away under trying circumstances. She could not think of anything to say to comfort her, so she said nothing, but let the widow do the talking. When she had to leave, the wife cried out, "Martha, you are the only one who has been any comfort to me. You were the first one I could talk to about Don." Martha had not said a thing, all she had done was listen.

Then last, be willing to take the time to pray with your friend. A heartbroken mother of a problem son just recently told how much she appreciated friends who would come and spend time with her in prayer for the boy. She could not understand the friends who were willing to give advice, but never would take time for prayer.

This is a tremendous ministry, the ministry of binding up broken hearts. The ability to comfort does not come to the lighthearted and merry. We must go down into the depths if we would experience this most precious of God's gifts—comfort—and thus be prepared to be co-workers together with Him.

Chapter 16

## *OUR STRANGE WAYS OF DEATH*

By Bob W. Brown
Henry A. Buchanan

Something is wrong with the American way of death. What is it? The costliness of funerals? Superstition? Pagan rites? Automated funeral parlors? Embalming? Cremation? Cadillac hearses and motorcycle escorts? Memorial gardens and perpetual care? Concrete vaults and stainless steel caskets?

No. These are only symptoms. The real trouble is that, even with the current wave of interest in the subject, Americans will not face up to the reality of death.

Take Anton, for instance. Everybody knew he was dying, but nobody would discuss it with him. When he asked his physician frankly, "Am I going to make it or not, Doc?" the doctor could only evade the issue. "I'm just seeing how you will respond to this new medicine," was his reply. Twice Anton tried to talk to his wife, but she brushed him off. "You mustn't talk like that," she said nervously. "Everything's going to be all right." When Anton's pastor tried to visit, he was intercepted at the door. "Just make it seem that you're here on a routine call," he was told. "If Anton thinks we called you, it will upset him."

Then when Anton did die, his wife became hysterical. "No! No!" she screamed. "He can't be dead. I won't believe it! What is going to become of me?"

"Get hold of yourself!" her brother gently scolded. "Anton wouldn't want you acting that way."

The ward clerk called the chaplain and asked him to come and see if he could do anything with the family. Just as he arrived, a nurse also came in with a hypodermic needle for the wife. "The doctor ordered this for you to help you relax," she explained.

The minister offered a brief prayer, while the distraught woman snuffled quietly on her brother's shoulder. Then she began convulsing with grief. "Oh God!" she screamed. And turning her dilated eyes on the minister she demanded, "Why would God take my husband away from me? What am I going to do without him?" Then she subsided. The hypo had begun to take effect.

Even though the taboo on death is being lifted, we still have a hard time facing it when we see it coming. The temptation is to deny it. But that is cruel for the one who is dying. By refusing to admit it, we make it impossible for him to say goodbye. By trying to disguise his condition, we isolate him from the very people he needs most. We raise an impossible barrier between ourselves and him. And yet we know that the charade can't go on forever.

The natural reaction to death is grief, a full surrender to the mental agony and the emotional suffering which has been brought on by the severing

## Our Strange Ways of Death

of ties that were deep and meaningful. But here again, we try to escape it. Unless grief is allowed to run a normal course—even a seemingly excessive one at times—serious emotional consequences can follow. Outbursts of grief, in themselves upsetting and disturbing to the other person, should not be confused with the problem. They are a part of the solution to the problem.

Yet it is difficult to stand by the bereaved person without yielding to the impulse to relieve their grief in some way. Doctors and nurses mean well when they administer drugs, and in some cases they may indeed be necessary. But drugs can become a substitute for that peace which comes only through acceptance of the necessity and the painfulness of grief.

Claire, a woman in her seventies, was frantic. Her husband had dropped to the floor during a routine visit to his doctor. He had been whisked away to the hospital, where he was pronounced dead on arrival. She had followed, but now was told that she could not go into the room where he lay. She wrung her hands in agony.

A nurse tried to sedate her, but she refused, saying, "I don't want to go to sleep." Her refusal was considered irrational, and her request to see her dead husband was deemed very unwise. Yet what could be *more* normal in view of the shock she had sustained? Her desire to see her husband's body was a perfectly natural one, and her refusal to accept a sedative was an indication of her strength.

After death comes burial. The funeral ritual itself, often criticized as "pagan," plays an important role in the grief process. It enables the survivors to make death more acceptable. It gives a certain dignity to the parting. Men of all ages and all cultures have ritualized their deepest feelings—their loves, their fears and their guilts. In the ritual of death all these feelings are expressed.

Most of the fuss and expense of the funeral involves the preparation and disposal of the corpse. Consequently this has become a prime target of criticism. Is our apparent preoccupation with the body really pagan? Do we dishonor the Spirit by our accent on the body? Not necessarily. Some of the most valid insights of the Christian faith are directly associated with the human body. Created as a temple of the spirit, the body of man can not be dissociated from the man himself. Not in life, nor in death.

The uniqueness of the Christian hope is not immortality of the soul but resurrection of the body. Whatever theological meaning this may have for people—and it may run the gamut from a strictly literal to a purely spiritual interpretation—it is humanly impossible for us to separate our appreciation of a person we have known from our memory of his bodily appearance. This is the way we experience the persons who are close enough to us for us to honestly grieve at their deaths.

To most people the body is not only the vehicle for the expression of personality; it is almost synonymous with the person himself. The respectful treatment accorded the bodies of the dead is an expression of respect for human personality itself. It is a way of saying that man himself has value. Disrespect for the body of the dead reflects a lack of respect for the man's life.

The ancient Egyptians built the pyramids to entomb the embalmed bodies of their pharaohs. An exaggerated emphasis on the body? Yes. But in this way the glories of a powerful civilization were preserved and have become the common heritage of the human race. A slab of granite on Grandpa's grave is no less significant to his heirs who return to read the inscription which witnesses that he lived and died.

There *is* something wrong with funeral and burial practices in America today. This "something wrong" is that we have attempted to remove all personal responsibility for these rites and thereby to remove the fact of death from our personal experiences. Due to our increasing urbanization, the movement of people to a few metropolitan centers, we have lost not only our roots in the simple rural community where everybody joined in the mourning and the burial of one of its members; we have even lost our burying grounds.

Thirty or forty years ago church membership meant burial privileges in the cemetery on church property. Families arriving at church for worship services regularly went to the cemetery to place fresh flowers on the graves of their loved ones, and once each year the congregation gathered for the express purpose of cleaning up the cemetery. Children often played among the tombstones, read the inscriptions and became familiar with the fact of death—and assumed some responsibility for keeping the graves.

The net effect of this was good, just as the net effect of the primitive funeral with its free expression of grief was good. Emotional difficulties arise in human beings when they try to slough off the earthy and primitive expressions of their deeply-felt emotional needs without providing an adequate substitute for the old ways.

What we have today is a pseudo-sophistication—people trying to convince themselves and others that they do not have the feelings and the needs which a more primitive and more honest culture experienced in the face of death. The church parking lot has taken the place of the church cemetery, and the psychiatrist's couch must substitute for the open expression of grief.

Our large city churches must develop new concepts, new attitudes and new programs to cope with the problem. Clergymen and church leaders must find adequate ways for people to express their grief in a religious context and to identify personally with the experience of death and the responsibilities which the death of one member places on those who remain alive. Even these demands need not bring forth anything essentially new, but only more adaptable channels for the age-old, time-tested waters of grief.

When John F. Kennedy died, the nation suspended its normal activities and for three days mourned the death of its leader. Not only did the dignitaries of the world attend the funeral at the church in the nation's capital, but the American people followed—on TV—the horse-drawn caisson to Arlington Cemetery and watched the slain president laid to rest. The millions of grief-stricken spectators became participants in the terrible drama of death as they identified themselves with the courageous woman who walked beside her husband's bier. By the hundreds of thousands they still come to the place where they laid him, where an eternal flame stands as a monument to the life of a man snuffed out by an assassin's bullets. The whole nation may well be grateful that a way was

## Our Strange Ways of Death

found to express the grief and shock which attend so tragic a death.

What is the role of the minister in the drama of human death? Is the cleric with his prayers and exhortations the useless vestige of superstitions that should have been buried with the corpse? Or does he actually bridge the yawning chasm between the living and the dead? In fact, either view may be a bit extreme. But the minister does have a unique place in mankind's struggle to face up to the implications of his mortality. Both because of what he is as a man, and what he symbolizes as a minister, he may become the human agent by which a bereaved person is able to transform his encounter with death from a defeat to a victory.

Often a minister may do most when he does seemingly nothing. If he is able to sit and grieve silently with the bereaved, that may do more good than volumes of well-meant exhortations. Just his presence is significant. And weeks afterward, the person who has regained his composure and confidence will say to him, "You'll never know what it meant to me for you to be there. I don't think I could have borne it without your help."

There are pitfalls in the funeral, but there are opportunities for growth, too. It is quite possible that with many people the dominant elements of grief are shame, resentment and embarrassment rather than love and sympathy for the dead relative. If they can find in the words or in the attitude of the minister something that will help them to forgive, to recover their own self-respect and to move ahead into life with a positive appreciation for what is left to them, not only has the pitfall been escaped, but the opportunity has been seized.

The only thing surer than death is life itself. But

to realize life's promise, a man must face the reality of death—for himself as well as for his loved ones. Dodging the issue, or camouflaging it in some way, only robs both the dying and the bereaved of a potentially rich and meaningful experience.

Chapter 17

## *DON'T SHORT-CIRCUIT GRIEF*

By Robert James St. Clair

The pastor was smiling.

"You don't look like a man who has just returned from a funeral," I remarked.

"Nope," he said. "It was more like a revival. We had such freedom preaching the joy and the victory that I even thought of giving an altar call. I didn't, of course, but the devil got more than he bargained for."

It is hard to predict the ultimate result of that service. It may have provided comfort. We have abundant evidence, however, that the results of such an approach are often frustration and needless anxiety. The soul supposedly "comforted" by the good news of Christ's victory over the grave may find—months or even years later—that his comfort has worn thin. Depression, loneliness, intense hostility, and chronic fatigue break through, making life more trouble than it is worth.

Just as the hand which has lost a finger must have time to heal, so death is a cutting which must heal. There is no shortcut, no quick cure. It is cruelly naive to assume that a Christian's belief in the resurrection will spare him the grief of bereavement.

Hope and comfort in the face of death do spring from the heart of the Christian gospel. Jesus Christ did rise from the dead, and will likewise raise His own from the dead, and they will live together with Him forever. They will never again experience parting, or sorrow, or tears. But while this glorious hope can—and should—temper our sorrow here on this earth, it is not meant to eliminate it. We recover from grief by means of a healing process. The gospel of Christ can greatly augment that process or, if it is used as a short-circuit, it can seriously delay and distort it.

Ever since Dr. Erich Lindemann began his work on grief after the Coconut Grove fire in 1943, intensive studies have been conducted on the whole process of bereavement and comfort. We now realize that there are several predictable phases which God, the Creator, has built into the grief process. A person who is aware of them will be able to comfort a grieving friend or relative more effectively by making careful allowance for each stage. Not everyone goes through precisely the same stages, or spends the same amount of time in each stage. But every grieving person must go through them, if he is to emerge a whole person afterwards.

(1) The first phase is shock. It may be hardly noticeable in some, but this does not mean they are escaping it. They may show little emotion, but what they are actually doing is denying the whole thing. The loss is so great that only by denying it can they keep themselves from shattering. Others will cry out immediately. But in either case, the whole personality is reacting to the horror of hav-

## Don't Short-Circuit Grief

ing an intimate part of life cut off. The heart must bleed.

(2) The second stage is bodily distress. As the bereaved person goes through the turbulence of emotional upheaval, he may experience fleeting physical aches and pains as well. Or he may actually adopt the illness of the one gone, as if he were becoming one again with someone "who never should have left." We can safely assume, I think, that no one would bluntly say, "Why, snap out of it. This sickness is all in your head." It hardly comforts a sick person to be told that he is really incapacitated by his imagination.

(3) During the third stage, the person experiences a marked loss of enjoyment for anything. For awhile he may slavishly adhere to his daily routine, making each activity a project in itself. But he is restless, and moves in an erratic fashion. A lot of time just seems to be lost; he has no real zest for anything.

(4) In the fourth stage, an abundance of conflicting and hidden emotions emerge as Depression. An ominous cloud hides the sun. The grieving spirit begins weeping at any moment. Sadness becomes an intolerable load. The fleeting thought of suicide comes, leaving the soul terrified. Nothing makes sense, nothing is worth doing, and it is clear now that much of life was enjoyed because he could share it with someone else. Overly dependent persons may realize how much they had kept their center of gravity in a "stronger" person; they had tasted life vicariously. Now that their center of gravity is gone, what is left?

(5) It seems strange, but grief eventually leads to some form of guilt. Sometimes it is simply the realization that in a world of suffering we have

lived rather selfishly. Sometimes it gathers like drops of water into a small pool. Guilt begets guilt as one failure reminds us of others.

Mrs. V. heard her husband gasp, but ignored it, thinking he was just tired. When she finally came around to him, she discovered he was dying of a heart attack. To top it all off, she fumbled around attempting to contact a doctor, and an hour later he died. As the days wore on she felt black with worthlessness. Her dread ruminations raked up from her mind every failure, every neglect, every argument she ever had with her husband. She developed sharp pains in her chest and was prepared to die of a heart attack. The doctors could find nothing organically wrong. She was drowning in a pool of remorse.

(6) With guilt such as this, hostility can't be far behind. We tend to feel angry with people who have made us feel guilty. But if we don't realize that, we are apt to turn our anger on others instead. And so the grieving person vacillates between anger turned inward, and anger turned outward—toward the doctor for poor treatment, the pastor for poor ministry, the nurses for poor attention, and relatives for inconsiderate behavior. Or, he may turn his anger on God. Often a person apparently angry at a particular church or church member is covering up a much deeper anger towards God, who he feels is ultimately responsible for the whole parade of horrors in his life. Then years later, if this anger is not dealt with, depression may be triggered out of all proportion by a loss not nearly as severe as the previous one.

To complicate the matter, a devout person may feel guilty about feeling angry. And it doesn't help when a "comforter" comes and tries to talk him

## Don't Short-Circuit Grief

out of his feelings. His glib preachments only generate more anger as they ride roughshod over the integrity of the person's emotions. But how can he say anything when someone is reading the Scriptures and praying over him? How many grieving persons have gotten bogged down in this stage, simply for lack of proper understanding and counsel!

(7) At some point there comes a resistance to continuing life as usual. It seems an outrage to resume business as before, as if death made no difference. The bereaved person smolders with resentment that others can be so callous as to engage in their usual activities, as though life had not caved in after all. He postpones major enterprises, omits the yearly vacation, neglects associations he had shared with the deceased, and falters in social duties for which they had been responsible together.

(8) The mourner is rounding out the healing process when he is able to absorb reality and participate once again in demanding activities. Thoughts continue to haunt, dreams return, and scars remain. But now he senses that life does not stop because of death. Life involves death, greets it, communicates with it daily, but it goes on. Because Christ is alive, death dies and life remains. Change and decay is in all we see, so that our hearts might be attuned to the abiding life of God.

What can we do to cooperate with God as He heals the broken-hearted? It is His work, and will progress only under the guidance of His Spirit. This means several things to us.

(1) It is harmful to arrest the mourner's thoughts by long Scriptures, many small sermons and long, long prayers. Why is it, that in moments of anxiety so many of us attempt to establish security by raising the flag of orthodoxy and reciting

the correct phrases? "For the kingdom of God does not consist in talk but in power" (I Cor. 4:20). Squelch the need to wrest control of the situation by profound speeches. Your handshake and your presence speak with eloquence.

(2) Love is God's response to man's sense of frailty. You can show love best by listening. You may feel that the mourner's lengthy recounting of so many past events, often accompanied by tears, is harmful. Not so. If he tried to forget everything immediately, it would cause him untold harm later in life. It helps him to know that you care enough to share these events, and it will take discipline on your part to listen attentively to what may sound like endless repetition. But you stand for reality and for life! You offer love! You are giving him support as his tearful heart slowly absorbs the fact that in this life, at least, someone is gone.

(3) Do not be shocked by whatever the grief-stricken person says. It is impossible to sort out rationally his turbulent emotions. Later he may wish to apologize for acting irrationally, for seeming to deny Christ, or for expressing hostility. He needs to realize that you quite understand that not all phases of healing are pleasant. Death is a nightmare of brutality and God has given us every right to weep and be shocked. His greatest comfort to us is ours to offer, "I will be with you."

(4) Let the bereaved decide how he wishes you to participate in this healing. If he wishes the Bible read or a prayer offered, do so in a concise, restrained manner. If he has a preferred passage, read it without a lengthy sharing of your own grief experiences.

(5) The pastor ministering in the funeral service will do well to avoid sentimentality and eulo-

gies. Painting impressions of those with whom others have had to live a lifetime irritates wounds and aggravates conflicting feelings. A simple statement of the mighty acts of God in Christ, together with familiar passages from the Word of God, provide ample opportunity for God's work in the heart.

(6) Let us take up again the practice of the funeral dinner. In this rite, the women prepare a simple meal at the church or the home. After the service the family gathers to eat and to talk over old times. It is amazing how meaningful this is, this seeing and feeling everyone together. Conversation buzzes, occasionally there is laughter, and we are not alone. Even while some are dwelling on the past, they see by gentle reminder that there is for them still more work to do and more precious memories to create. It is also a reminder that one day all chairs will be filled again, and Christ's family circle will be unbroken.

(7) Finally, pastor and close friends have a valuable function. By their contacts they must be alert to the first signs that the bereaved is ready to take up a new day. Nothing hurried. Smaller tasks, then heavier ones. It comes as something of a reluctant surprise that after death we can go on again. At first we are grieved at the pains God permits. Later we are reverently grateful for the provisions He has made. It appears that this darkness has served to bring us closer to the dayspring of the life eternal.

Chapter 18

# TWO VIEWS ON TODAY'S FUNERAL CUSTOMS:
## I. SORROWING AS THOSE WHO HAVE HOPE

By ROGER F. CAMPBELL

CUSTOMS ARE strange things. They seem so right when in use, but often appear equally odd after they have been abandoned.

Funeral customs are no exception.

Consider a few examples.

It was the practice in Ireland, at one time, to remove all nails from the top of the coffin at the end of the funeral so that the dead would have no difficulty in freeing themselves on the day of the resurrection. Also, the shroud or winding sheet was often loosened from the feet and hands, lest its tight folds should prevent a speedy exit at that moment.

In some areas it was common for those near death to sleep in a casket, so they would feel comfortable after death came.

In Sweden a mirror was buried with unmarried women so that they might arrange their loosely coiled tresses and be in good appearance at the resurrection. The married women wore their hair in braids, making the mirror unnecessary for them.

An interesting evidence of man's idea that he

could carry something material into eternity was the Russian custom of placing a parchment "Certificate of Good Conduct" in the hands of the deceased. It was thought that he could present this as a credential to assure ready entrance into heaven.

The Romans buried their children under the eaves of their houses so the infant spirit would not wander about.

Until the year 1829, the awful rite of self-immolation was common in India. In this gruesome custom the widow voluntarily perished in the flames of the funeral pyre at the death of her husband.

The tombs of kings have yielded the bodies of wives, servants, animals, and sometimes even pastors (perish the thought), all having been buried with the king to give him assistance and companionship after death.

A display of grief at the funeral was once considered proof of the importance of a man. For that reason, paid mourners often increased the volume of weeping and the duration of public grief.

Herodotus even describes the breaking of the foreleg of the dead man's horse, so the poor animal would have an appearance of sorrow at the loss of his master. The Turks put mustard seed in the horse's nostrils so that he would shed tears in the presence of the guests at the funeral.

In America, the customs of Roman Catholic, Jewish, and Protestant funerals have some major differences in form, with a number of minor variations within each group.

The Catholic funeral usually begins at the funeral home with the casket open and a very brief service. This is followed by a procession to the church where the casket remains closed. There is then another procession to the cemetery for committal.

Jewish burial is carried out within twenty four hours of death, if possible. Clothing for the deceased is very plain so as not to show a difference between the rich and the poor. Another service is often held a year after the funeral at the unveiling of a stone marker for the grave.

Protestant funerals are generally on the third day after death, and the service is held at a funeral home or at a church with a brief graveside or chapel service following.

In most cases, there is visitation at the funeral home with an open casket, between the time of death and the funeral. Often the casket remains open through the funeral service and is closed just before the procession to the cemetery.

If it had not been for the request of one Christian lady, I might have gone through my ministry thinking that funeral customs were like the laws of the Medes and Persians that could not be altered. She left instructions for her funeral. They were as follows:

1. There was to be no funeral service before going to the cemetery.
2. There would be a graveside service with a closed casket.
3. There would be a memorial service later that day.

Strange, I thought! I guess I even chafed a bit under this break with tradition. Yet, after conducting too many funerals in the score of years since that "different" one, I would still choose her order of service for my own.

Another woman who has questioned current funeral practices is the one I married. She informed

## Sorrowing as Those Who Have Hope

me long ago that she did not want her friends to have their last look at her in death. She said she wanted to be remembered *alive*. At first I thought it was just female vanity, but the more I thought about it the better it sounded.

Alive! What a good word! And what a good way to be remembered!

Influenced, then, by two ladies who have dared choose something other than tradition, and by personal experience in sharing the sorrows of death with hundreds of others, I now question some of the customs of our way of death.

Consequently, I offer the following suggestions:

*When death comes, call your pastor before calling the funeral director.*

This is not to cast any reflections upon the undertaker's profession, nor the men in it. I have found most of them to be gracious and thoughtful. But, that first call to the pastor does set your priorities right. It demonstrates that you value spiritual help above everything else. Another advantage is that of receiving your pastor's counsel as to funeral procedure before you are swept along with the traditional order of things.

*Consult your pastor about a Christian Memorial.*

Thousands of dollars are spent on flowers that could be channeled to the outreach of the gospel. Here is opportunity for your loved one to have another witness, even after death. But you must act quickly! This decision must be made in time for your funeral director to notify the newspaper of your desire. Don't worry about a floral tribute, for many will send flowers in spite of your request.

*Consider keeping the casket closed during visitation.*

It is at this point that you will encounter difficulty. Now you are moving against the tide of tradition. Your funeral director will probably not approve. Friends and family are certain to be perplexed, and will urge you to change your mind. You may wonder if it is worth the effort, but I feel confident you will find that the rewards outweigh the problems.

Every person who questions the closed casket provides another opportunity to explain that your loved one is in heaven.

A picture showing the departed Christian in days of health will assist in remembering him as he was while living. Good memories will become the topic of conversation, rather than the long illness of recent years, or the tragic accident. The whole mood will be changed and lifted.

Most important, you will be living the truth that others quote: "We are confident, I say, and willing rather to be absent from the body, and to be present with the Lord" (II Cor. 5:8).

Let it be clear that this suggestion does not rule out embalming or preparation for burial. You may even want a brief family viewing, or, out of Christian compassion, a private viewing for friends or loved ones who may not understand or be able to accept the fact of death. You are simply eliminating the illusion of friends visiting a Christian after his death; for that is impossible apart from a future meeting in heaven.

*Keep the casket closed during the funeral.*

The funeral of a Christian is a great opportunity for preaching the gospel, but an open casket may hinder the effectiveness of the message. It is almost impossible to get the attention of a mourner whose eyes are fixed on the body of a departed friend or loved one. Words of comfort, so desperately needed, are often completely missed because the hearers are consumed with grief.

An open casket also invites a final farewell; another grief wrenching ritual that suggests the "departed" has not yet really departed. Sometimes, in desperate desire to help a grieving family tarrying in their last look, I have longed to shout the words the angel gave at the resurrection of Jesus: "He is not here!" How much better to have the casket closed while the pastor emphasizes the truth of an immediate arrival in heaven!

*Give thought to a memorial service instead of a funeral.*

What's the difference? A memorial service usually follows the service at the cemetery, while a funeral precedes it. The funeral stresses the ending of life. A memorial service can be given to sharing the impact of a Christian witness. A funeral service speaks of finality. A Christian memorial service glories in the blessings of the past and anticipates reunion in the future. I think it is worthy of consideration.

*Today's funeral customs: How Christian are they?*

You will have to be the judge of that, as the Lord leads you in your time of grief. At that time you may produce better alternatives than any I have suggested. I hope so.

Don't forget that any move against established tradition is risky and may bring criticism. But, for the Christian, there is a greater danger, that of being tied to traditions that make the Word of God of no effect.

## II. *A TIME TO MOURN*

### By Eleanor Harker

"FUNERAL FOPPERY" — that's how Charles Haddon Spurgeon described it. And there have even been many secular books written decrying the whole business (and a lucrative business it is).

But of course Christians today also have their doubts about the American way of death. Roger Campbell presents one attempt to examine the merits of separating ourselves from usual death customs which many would judge nothing short of pagan. There is much to commend Campbell's observations. And five years ago before my mother died I would have probably been in almost total agreement with his view. But now I know there's another side to the story.

Campbell offers an alternate order of services after the pattern of one Christian lady he has known. Again, there may be positive value to this departure from usual custom. Not bothering with a viewing would certainly seem to cut down the wear and tear on the grieving family, for one thing.

But I'm not sure the wear and tear is damaging,

## A Time to Mourn

at least not in all cases. From my own experience I can testify that the traditional viewing and funeral procedures gave me—at a time when empty hours would have been devastating—a structure, a busyness, an involvement with people which helped ease me gradually into a more acute period of grief later on. Those three or four days of activity provided a buffer zone before the stark reality of loss set in.

There are also things to be said in favor of the open casket. In his discussion of this point Campbell quotes his wife as saying that "she did not want her friends to have their last look at her in death. She said she wanted to be remembered *alive*." He also says that if you opt for a closed casket "a picture showing the departed Christian in days of health will assist in remembering him as he was while living." And it is suggested that "for friends or loved ones who may not understand or be able to accept the fact of death" you may have to conduct a brief private viewing of the body.

There is something very wrong with this whole line of reasoning. First of all, seeing my mother in death does not prevent me from also remembering her aliveness. It is not a question of either/or—it's both. It's a question of seeing reality whole—reality in a fallen world where death is still a fact and will be until Jesus comes again.

And if we do not want to look at a body in a casket in order that we can keep *only* our good healthful memories—well then, we'd also better stay away from the dying person in his last days in the hospital too! After all, why should my last look at my mother alive conjure up the painful memory of a swollen discolored body breathing so hard she almost sounded like a neighing horse? She seemed so relieved to see the whole family come be with her the night she died—but maybe she should have insisted we all stay home so we could remember her in better days. Or maybe we should have just chosen to stay home. Obviously these comments are absurd and un-Christian.

A photograph of the person when he/she was alive and well also promotes a fantasy. Perhaps an open casket can sometimes falsely suggest that "the 'departed' has not really departed." But doesn't a healthy picture do the same thing? That person in the photograph, even though he is with the Lord, no longer exists *in that particular form and likeness* and he never will again.

Furthermore, it is my contention that those who are unable to face the fact of death are often the same people who are unable to look at the body in the casket.

One lady who came to the viewing stands out in my mind. She cast a quick glance in the direction of the casket, winced, and turned away. I do not mean to be harshly critical of her, because death does hurt. But since then, in my acquaintance with her, I have seen that this woman's ability to face other hard situations is limited.

This, of course, is not conclusive proof of anything, but Joseph Bayly, in his book, *The View from a Hearse* (David C. Cook), seems to confirm my amateur psychological observations: "Expert opinion seems to be that immediate comprehension and acceptance of the reality of the loss and immediate expression of grief are most helpful in recovering from the shock of death's separation and moving forward in life. . . .

"This is why viewing the body in its casket is not condemned as a barbaric procedure for survivors.

## A Time to Mourn

These hours with the corpse before burial prove the finality of death's separation to many people as nothing else could."

Of course, when Bayly speaks of the finality of death's separation he is operating in the context of this temporal life. But until we get to heaven separation *is* final, and, as the quote suggests, if we don't face that fact a really fruitful moving forward in life will be thwarted.

Paul Irion, a leading authority on funerals in the American church, says much the same thing in his book, *The Funeral: Vestige or Value?* (Abingdon). He is opposed to the concept of memorial services without the body of the deceased because it avoids a frank facing of reality.

I know for me that not only looking at the body, but also the shock of touching it (and that's the fact—*it*, not her) utterly convinced me that the real part of my mother, her spirit, had departed, as no mere teaching could have. That cold stiff form may have looked familiar but in reality bore no resemblance to the *person* I had known. I knew she was gone.

Campbell also maintains that if you have a closed casket "good memories will become the topic of conversation, rather than the long illness of recent years, or the tragic accident." However, I did not find that an open casket really hindered the flow of happy anecdotes. Many people related special instances of mother's kindness in years past. Funny occasions, and especially many meaningful notes she had written which people had especially kept and treasured over the years were usual topics of conversation. And in our case, many of her acquaintances were virtually unknown to us; she taught in an elementary school in an area some

10-to-15 minutes away. Those people would have never felt close enough to the family to come visit and share their remembrances in our home. I remember during the viewing my sister-in-law said, "I've really learned a lot." And I did too.

In fact, this is one advantage of having a separate, evening time for a viewing. Services, either at the graveside, funeral home or church are not as conducive for chatting and visiting as is a viewing setting. And as services are usually held during the day, many people find it hard to get time off from work to attend.

Finally, Campbell says, "Sometimes, in desperate desire to help a grieving family tarrying in their last look, I have longed to shout the words the angel gave at the resurrection of Jesus: 'He is not here!' "

A teary child I know of was chided at the funeral of her grandfather. "Don't you know he's in heaven?" someone asked her. "Yes, I know he's in heaven," she replied, "but *I'm not*." And that's the point. We are left behind to go on living, and it's not selfish or un-Christian to indicate emotionally that this person was so valuable and significant in our lives that he/she will be greatly missed. We are to "sorrow not, even as others which have no hope." But as Bayly says, there is a legitimate "hopeful sorrow." There is "a time to weep, and a time to laugh; a time to mourn, and a time to dance."

Let's not minimize the trauma of death. We are free enough as believers to experience every event in life honestly and fully. But praise God that beyond whatever painful moments life here holds we can look forward to the day when God Himself will wipe all tears from our eyes.

Chapter 19

# *HOW CHRISTIAN ARE OUR FUNERALS?*

By Frances Tucker

AN OLD MAN stood up to give a testimony in a small country church. The light of the sun was in his deep bronze features, the light of Christ's peace in his eyes: "Let not your heart be troubled," he quoted, "I go to prepare a place for you and if I go to prepare a place for you, I will come again and receive you unto myself; that where I am, there ye may be also."

"I thank God," he said, "that I am ready for Him when He comes."

Two weeks later town residents filed into the same church for his funeral. His lifeless form rested in a lavish coffin which had put his family in debt for many months. During fifteen minutes of the funeral service, plaintive music accompanied somber poetry, read by the minister. The dead man's family sat not more than two feet from the open coffin, listening to intermittent sobbing of those about them, trying to maintain a Christian testimony. As the eulogy was given, summarizing the finer details of his life, sobs were more frequent and tears more profuse. At the close of the half-hour service, a line of people moved slowly by the casket. Several women became hysterical upon looking into the face of the deceased.

On whose behalf were tears shed? Certainly not for the radiant old man who had rejoiced to see his Savior. One message he would have desired at his funeral: "For God so loved the world that He gave His only begotten Son that whosoever believeth in Him should not perish, but have everlasting life."

For whose benefit was the lavish coffin ordered? Not for the old man's. He had been interested in a Christian college and gave it five dollars a month from a meagre pension to help train Christian youth. Wouldn't he have preferred to see the thousands of dollars spent on his funeral given to this Christian work?

How many of our funeral customs are derived from our Christian faith? They often seem to be more pagan than Christian, and a close examination of them even confuses the pagan.

A missionary once remonstrated with a native because he had put some rice on a new grave.

"Why do you put rice on the grave?" asked the missionary. "The dead cannot eat the rice."

Quickly the native responded. "Some time ago I saw you put flowers on another missionary's grave. Why? The dead cannot smell, can they?"

A Christian who wishes to honor Christ in the way he arranges or handles a funeral should anticipate the decisions he must make now, before he has to make them under an emotional strain. Here are some suggestions to consider:

(1) Upon the death of a loved one, call your minister. As a servant of God, he is trained to bring comfort from the Scriptures. Once your heart has

## How Christian Are Our Funerals?

been quieted, you will be better prepared to make the necessary decisions.

(2) Ask your minister to recommend a funeral director and, if possible, to assist you in making the funeral arrangements. He will know which directors are honest and which are not. Many will suggest that your love for the deceased will show itself in a costly funeral. But don't be led into debt by pleas that this is your last tribute to your loved one. As a believer, you know that your loved one's soul is not affected or impressed by an ornate casket. One minister states: "I like to remember that God takes as good care of the soul of the Christian who dies in a flaming airplane, or who is lost at sea, as He does of the person whose body is embalmed and placed in an airtight casket."

(3) Consider sealing the casket of your loved one before the funeral. In the past, this idea has been associated with emaciated bodies, suicides, and family secrets. But perhaps it would be a tribute to our faith if it were to become associated with Christians too. The Scriptures teach us that the body is only our "earthly tabernacle." It is not the real "us." When a Christian dies, he is then "absent from the body and present with the Lord" (II Cor. 5:8). The corpse is truly only the remains. If friends or relatives express a desire to see the body, encourage them to visit the funeral parlor or your home before the day of the funeral. One minister explained it this way: "In the presence of an open casket, the family will find it difficult, if not impossible, to ponder the Christian hope of resurrection. The open casket, while it might display the embalmer's skill, does not help us concentrate on the reality of eternal life. On more than one occasion I have seen a company of mourners reconciled

134  DEATH: JESUS MADE IT ALL DIFFERENT

and comforted during a service, only to become distraught moments later as they made their way to the open casket to look again at the corpse."

(4) Plan a funeral which will honor Christ and will cause you the least amount of distress. Consider just a short committal service at the grave, instead of a formal church service. (A memorial service could be held in the church later, if desired.) Surely, such a service with only close friends and relatives gathered at the grave, and the family pastor reading from God's Word, could be satisfactory to many Christians. It need last only fifteen minutes, and would not be the emotional drain on the family that a large funeral would be. If you prefer a more formal funeral, and the deceased was a true believer, honor the Lord by having it in a church. Many ministers feel that poetry destroys the strength of the Gospel testimony at a funeral and upsets people emotionally. So consider having the pastor read just Scripture, with few comments, except to assure the believer of eternal life through Christ, and to testify to the unbeliever of salvation through the death of Christ.

(5) Consider asking your friends and relatives to express their sympathy in "living memorials," instead of flowers. One minister reports that he has conducted funerals where $2,000 to $3,000 was spent for flowers. By way of contrast, the chapel furniture in the education building of the Warren Park Church in Chicago is there because the Rev. John Hess's wife requested living memorials for her husband. Many thousands of dollars have been given for educational scholarships as families request "living memorials" in place of flowers. How great is the need of our Bible institutes and Christian colleges!

Hold a family discussion on these issues. As a believer in the risen Christ you will not shun this subject. Find out how your loved ones feel about simple caskets, closed caskets, and "living memorials." If you discuss these matters now, no funeral director will convince you later that you are dishonoring the memory of your loved one by a particular decision you may make.

When we are born in a Christian family, our parents commit us to the Lord, either by a baptismal service or dedication. These services last only a few minutes, as the parents rejoice in the Lord over the life He has sent. When God chooses to call that life back to Him, ought not our sorrow to be in dignity, brevity, and peaceful worship?

Consider now what you will do with regard to the funeral, committal, casket, and memorials. Before those first lonely hours after God has called your loved one Home, make decisions which will honor the Savior you love.

## Chapter 20

# *GRANDMA'S FUNERAL: PAINFUL POSTMORTEM*

By Bruce R. Reichenbach

It is two months now since she died. She passed away peacefully, they said. She experienced no pain—at least in the end. Of course, no one will ever know the excruciating agony she underwent in her last years of old age: the headaches, dizziness, shortness of breath and sundry other pains. But she's dead now—at least she died peacefully.

The death of my wife's grandmother was the first death that really touched me, for my own grandparents died while I was still a boy. But her death set me to thinking, to pondering what meaning death might have for me, the living. Is death more than an event undergone by the deceased? Can it be a revelation to the living of their own selves?

Her death wasn't a shock, really; we knew it would happen sooner or later. That it happened when it did was not really the disturbing issue. Rather, my disturbance was caused by my own failures in my relationship with her, due largely to that very human trait: putting off until later for the sake of self's ease.

## Grandma's Funeral: Painful Postmortem

We knew she was very sick. The Hong Kong flu had led to pneumonia. We discussed visiting her. But eastern Michigan is so very far from Minnesota, a good day's drive. And we would have to sacrifice time needed for studying and work. So we waited and called her again, and were cheered by her seeming recovery. Yes, we would be sure to see her this summer.

As I stood by the casket, I wondered how sad she must feel that she had not seen us before she died. Oh yes, she no longer knew that, or could feel sad, but somehow if only.... She would surely have wanted to see us, to visit with us. It would make such a difference to her. But it really makes no difference now either way: she's dead. All her past is forgotten, especially by her. What difference could a past visit make now; she no longer knows anything. And yet . . .

We made the long day's trip to see her dead. She does not know it, and it really does not matter to her. We remember but she does not; we know we "sacrificed" our time to come but she does not. We made the long, tedious trip to visit the dead—why not to visit the living? True, even if we had made the visit two weeks earlier, it would make no difference to her now—she's dead. But somehow, that little fact does not seem to ease the feeling of guilt, of remorse. For the point really seems to be that we failed her in life. We could have meant so much to her, have touched her and her us. We could have brought mental, if not physical, healing. We could have brought joy, if only momentary, to a *person*. We could have relished the living; instead we reverenced the dead.

The issue here is simple. We loved ourselves, our security, our money, our ease better than we loved her. We "sacrificed" the very same things to make an appearance at her funeral; would it not have been infinitely more valuable to have made a sacrifice for the living? Perhaps death can teach us that relating to the living is intrinsically more valuable than mourning the dead, that life manifested in persons (whatever eternal value it also has) must be faced on its here and now basis. It is the present relationships which matter *now*.

Then there was the funeral. Grandmother never had much when she was alive. She worked incredibly long hours almost up to the end. Her home was a clean but crowded trailer, twenty feet by eight, with an old stove that refused to produce anything less than eighty degree heat. Her bed had all the lumps a mattress could safely hold. Her clothes were old—why did she need new ones? Who would know—or see—or care? And she never had the fifty dollars to fix her hot water heater that froze during the winter, so she had to heat on the stove all the hot water she used.

But there she lay, snuggled in satin, the soft, pink kind she could never afford to enjoy while she was alive. And the casket, a gleaming, decorated bronze one, was shiny and new. When did she last have something so shiny and new to catch her fascinated gaze? Five, ten years ago? We gave her a lovely, expensive coffin to top off a poverty-stricken existence. We were generous with the money for the tombstone—indeed it cost more than all of the last three Christmas gifts combined. She has luxury now—but she's dead and cannot know.

Few ever deferred to her when she was alive. Yet in the funeral parlor the voices that once argued with her and shouted her down scarcely reached a

## Grandma's Funeral: Painful Postmortem

whisper. The highest pitch was the sickly soft hum of the electric organ.

Then there were the cars that slowed and pulled off the road as the black hearse moved ever so slowly to the hillside cemetery. When she was alive, these same deferring drivers would have unhesitatingly crowded her off the road if she but dared to get in the way of them and their all-important progress. Horns would have blared had she ventured to go as slowly as even twice the speed of the moving hearse.

Were not our values awry? Was not this truly a "transvaluation of values"? The conduct of deference (selflessness), of giving for the sake of another's comfort, of reverence, was performed in painstakingly perfect pageantry for the dead, not for the living. For her unfeeling "comfort" we generously offered her the finest, smoothest satin; for her fitful, uneasy sleep, lumps for a mattress and old cold sheets for covers. For her corpsely rest we gave her shiny brass; for her unselfish love trinkets of tinsel, the little Christmas check to salve our conscience. To her stiffened face we deferred in silence; behind her living back we gossiped. A transvaluation of values indeed!

Then there was the funeral sermon. The minister, dressed in black, himself seemingly broken, slowly rose to eulogize her. What wonderful words of tribute to this woman—a woman he never knew. What praise bestowed—on a person to whom he had never spoken. Were we to be convinced by him? Did we need his kindly prodding to remember her, to recall her love? Was it for soothing that someone had to tell us what we knew? Was this for comfort?

What irony that the unknown should softly

address us about her who was the known, that he who could only be ignorant of the real truth tried to relive her true character. How irreverent for the stranger to comfort the estranged with the same generalities he used at his last funeral. Are we all platitudinously alike?

Finally, there was the glorious future promised her—to comfort us. The comfort was to be in the firm assurance he gave us that she was with God, for He was "the Resurrection and the Life." She was softly swept into the eternal presence of Him for Whom she had little or no concern on earth. The comforting words could not have been for her, for what happiness would eternal life with a Stranger bring? And what could he know, and what could he say that would influence the Almighty? Indeed, was it not too late to help her commence her spiritual journey?

She's dead now. We've divided up what little she had. What was valuable to her is either thrown or packed away. It is not intrinsically valuable to us. She is dead, but perhaps her death has a message for us, the living. "Your values," death says, "are turned upside down. You defer to the dead, but despise the living. You donate generously to the dead, but refuse comfort to the living. You eulogize the dead, but gossip to ruin and hurt those alive. You are suddenly concerned with the soul of the departed, but continually forget the spirit of those present. In short, you love the dead, and hate the living. Cannot I teach you at least this: it is to the living that you must respond: Let the dead bury the dead. Come, love your family, your neighbor, now!"

## *The Best in Health Books by*
# LINDA CLARK, BEATRICE TRUM HUNTER *and* CARLSON WADE

### *By Linda Clark*

- ☐ **Know Your Nutrition**
- ☐ **Cloth $5.95** ☐ **Paperback $3.50**
- ☐ **Face Improvement Through Exercise and Nutrition** — $1.75
- ☐ **Be Slim and Healthy** — $1.25
- ☐ **Go-Caution-Stop Carbohydrate Computer** — 95¢
- ☐ **Light on Your Health Problems** — $1.25
- ☐ **The Best of Linda Clark** — $3.50

### *By Beatrice Trum Hunter*

- ☐ **Whole Grain Baking Sampler**
- ☐ **Cloth $6.95** ☐ **Paperback $2.25**
- ☐ **Food Additives and Your Health** — $1.25
- ☐ **Fermented Foods and Beverages** — $1.25
- ☐ **Golden Harvest Prize Winning Recipes** (ed. by BTH) — $1.25
- ☐ **Food and Your Health** (Anthology ed. by BTH) — $1.25

### *By Carlson Wade*

- ☐ **Fats, Oils and Cholesterol** — $1.50
- ☐ **Vitamins and Other Supplements** — $1.25
- ☐ **Hypertension (High Blood Pressure) and Your Diet** — $1.50

*Buy them at your local health or book store or use this coupon.*

---

Keats Publishing, Inc. (P.O. Box 876), New Canaan, Conn. 06840    75-A

Please send me the books I have checked above. I am enclosing $_____ (add 35¢ to cover postage and handling). Send check or money order—no cash or C.O.D.'s please.

Mr/Mrs/Miss _____

Address _____

City _____ State _____ Zip _____

(Allow three weeks for delivery)

# THREE VOLUMES IN ONE...
# NEVER BEFORE IN PAPERBACK

## The Pivot INSPIRATION THREE LIBRARY

brings you the best of inspirational thought together in new, bargain-priced volumes for family enrichment. The larger type and convenient size, the choice of the best authors and selections, make each volume a shared adventure in wisdom and insight for young and old.

☐ **VOLUME ONE** contains *As A Man Thinketh* by James Allen; *Acres of Diamonds* by Russell Conwell; and *Essay on Self-Reliance* by Ralph Waldo Emerson. Special introduction by David Poling **$1.25**

☐ **VOLUME TWO** contains *The Greatest Thing In The World* by Henry Drummond; *The Song Of Our Syrian Guest* by William Allen Knight; and *The Practice Of The Presence of God* by Brother Lawrence. Special introduction by David Poling. **$1.25**

☐ **VOLUME THREE** contains three original anthologies of classic Christian thought: *The Wisdom of Martin Luther; The Wisdom of John Wesley; The Wisdom of John Calvin*. Selected and with a special introduction by David Poling. **$1.25**

☐ **VOLUME FIVE** contains three Christmas Classics: *The Story Of The Other Wise Man* by Henry Van Dyke; *A Christmas Carol* by Charles Dickens; and *A Gift Of the Magi* by O. Henry. Special introduction by David Poling **$1.25**

**Buy them at your bookstore or use this handy coupon**

---

Keats Publishing, Inc. P.O. Box 876  
212 Elm Street, New Canaan, Conn. 06840

74F

Please send the books checked above. I am enclosing $_____. (Check or money order—no currency, no C.O.D.'s, please.) If less than three books are ordered, add 25¢ for postage and handling. We pay postage and handling on three books or more. Allow two weeks for delivery.

Name_____

Address_____

City _____ State _____ Zip _____

# THE PIVOT FAMILY CLASSICS SERIES

## INEXPENSIVE EDITIONS...
## COMPLETE AND UNABRIDGED

- ☐ **ABIDE IN CHRIST** by Andrew Murray. The famous book in which the author writes about the true meaning of the words "abide in me." Introduction by William J. Petersen, editor of *Eternity* magazine. **95¢**

- ☐ **DAILY STRENGTH FOR DAILY NEEDS** by Mary W. Tileston. Each page, one for every day of the year, strikes a note of comfort and assurance for today, and hope and confidence for tomorrow. Treasured by countless readers for nearly a century, an endless source of insight and inspiration. **$1.25**

- ☐ **GOLD DUST** by Charlotte Yonge. Daily reminders of Divine love, brief but memorable restatements of the truths the heart knows but the mind may forget. A storehouse of faith and understanding for the whole family. **95¢**

- ☐ **IN HIS STEPS** by Charles M. Sheldon. A new edition of the most popular novel ever written, with an inspiring introduction by Donald T. Kauffman. **95¢**

- ☐ **IN TUNE WITH THE INFINITE** by Ralph Waldo Trine. Drawing on his inspired understanding of Scripture, the author points out the way to peace of mind, in one of the inspirational classics of all time. **$1.25**

- ☐ **KEPT FOR THE MASTER'S USE** by Frances Ridley Havergal. Twelve paths to participating in God's mighty promise, in a book of lasting inspiration and guidance. **95¢**

- ☐ **OF THE IMITATION OF CHRIST** by Thomas à Kempis. The most famous book of devotions in Christendom. Meditations on the life and teachings of Jesus and second only to the Bible as a guide and inspiration. **95¢**

- ☐ **THE PILGRIM'S PROGRESS** by John Bunyan. An exciting larger-than-life adventure story and a document of faith and inspiration. Introduction by Donald T. Kauffman. **95¢**

- ☐ **WHAT ALL THE WORLD'S A-SEEKING** by Ralph Waldo Trine. The one great principle of life and how it can be understood and used. A truly "how to" for those who will open themselves to the chance for joy and peace. **$1.25**

**Buy them at your bookstore or use this handy coupon**

---

Keats Publishing, Inc. P.O. Box 876
212 Elm Street, New Canaan, Conn. 06840

741

Please send the books checked above. I am enclosing $_____. (Check or money order—no currency, no C.O.D.'s, please.) If less than three books are ordered, add 25¢ for postage and handling. We pay postage and handling on three books or more. Allow two weeks for delivery.

Name _____

Address _____

City _____ State _____ Zip _____